MEN WHO MARCH AWAY
Poems of the First World War

By I. M. Parsons

★

THE PROGRESS OF POETRY
*An Anthology of verse
from Hardy to the Present Day*
(1936)

POETRY FOR PLEASURE
An Anthology for schools

MEN WHO MARCH AWAY

Poems of the
First World War

Edited with an Introduction by
I. M. PARSONS

CHATTO & WINDUS
LONDON

Published by
Chatto & Windus Ltd
40 William IV Street
London W.C.2
★
Clarke, Irwin & Co. Ltd
Toronto

ISBN 0 7011 1008 2

First published July 1965
Second impression 1965
Third impression 1966
Fourth impression 1968
Fifth impression 1972

Introduction, Selection and Notes
© I. M. Parsons, 1965

Acknowledgments for the use of copyright material
will be found on pages 11 and 12
which are hereby made part of this copyright page

Printed Photolitho in Great Britain
by Cox & Wyman Ltd,
London, Fakenham and Reading

CONTENTS

FOR
SHEILA DICKINSON

LIST OF AUTHORS AND POEMS

[7]

ACKNOWLEDGMENTS

Grateful thanks are due to the following for their kind permission to reprint the copyright poems included in these pages: Madame Catherine Guillaume for poems from *The Collected Poems of Richard Aldington*; the author's representatives and Sidgwick & Jackson Ltd. for the poem by Herbert Asquith from *Poems 1912–33*; Mrs. Basil Gray and The Society of Authors for poems by Laurence Binyon from *Collected Poems*; Edmund Blunden for poems from *Poems 1914–30* (Cobden-Sanderson) and *Poems of Many Years* (Wm. Collins & Co. Ltd.); the author's representatives, Sidgwick & Jackson Ltd., McClelland & Stewart Ltd., Toronto, and Dodd, Mead & Co., New York, for poems from *The Collected Poems of Rupert Brooke*, Copyright 1915 by Dodd, Mead & Co., Copyright 1943 by Edward Marsh; Miss D. E. Collins and Dodd, Mead & Co., New York, for poems from *Collected Poems of G. K. Chesterton*, Copyright 1932 by Dodd, Mead & Co.; and Miss Collins and Methuen & Co. Ltd. for the poem 'To the Unknown Warrior'; the Literary Trustees of Walter de la Mare and The Society of Authors for poems by Walter de la Mare; Mrs. Freeman for a poem by John Freeman from *Last Poems* (Macmillan & Co. Ltd.); Mr. Michael Gibson and Macmillan & Co. Ltd. for poems by Wilfrid Wilson Gibson from *Collected Poems 1905–25*; to the author, International Authors N.V., Horno N.V., Cassell & Co. Ltd. and Doubleday & Co. Inc., New York, for poems by Robert Graves; the author's family and Burns & Oates Ltd. for the poem by Julian Grenfell; Mr. Robert Gurney for the poem 'The Silent One' by Ivor Gurney; Mr. Robert Gurney and Hutchinson & Co. (Publishers) Ltd. for the poem 'The Bohemians' from *Poems* by Ivor Gurney; and Mr. Robert Gurney and Sidgwick & Jackson Ltd. for the poem 'To His Love' from *War Embers* by Ivor Gurney; the Trustees of the author's estate, Macmillan & Co. Ltd. and The Macmillan Company, New York, for poems from *The Collected Poems of Thomas Hardy*; the author's representatives and Sidgwick & Jackson Ltd. for poems by F. W. Harvey from *Gloucestershire Friends*; the author, *Punch* and Methuen & Co. Ltd. for the poem 'Beaucourt Revisited' from *The Bomber*

INTRODUCTION

This is a selection of poems about the 1914–18 war. Not all of them were written during the actual course of the war: some are retrospective; and though most of them are the work of men who took an active part in the fighting, a small but significant number is by older poets like Hardy, Yeats, D. H. Lawrence and Walter de la Mare, who were indirectly rather than directly involved. One or two, such as Fredegond Shove's *The Farmer*—one of the few imaginative attempts to bridge the gap between life at home and the terrible happenings in France—or Charlotte Mew's strange, uneven, but to me disturbingly original poem *The Cenotaph*, were written by women. In short, I have not restricted my choice to poems written within a given period, or by those who would nowadays be called 'combatants'. But believing as I do that more good poetry came out of World War I than is generally recognised, I have tried to make a representative selection of it. Of poems, that is to say, which would not have been written if that war had not happened.

Many years ago, when I edited an anthology of modern verse called 'The Progress of Poetry', I was taken to task by W. J. Turner for saying in my Introduction that I had tried to select poems representative of 'the best of the poets' who had been writing during the period covered by my book. By what means, he asked, did I presume to be able to distinguish 'the best' from the second best and the also rans? A fair question. For of course all value judgments are subjective. But if one is to be obliged to qualify every such judgment with the words 'in my opinion' or 'so I think', one is quickly going to become a bore. I hope therefore that the reader will accept it if I say at the outset that I have only included poems which *seem to me* to be valuable contributions to the literature of the first World War, and will thereafter take the italicized words for granted.

It is necessary to say this, because having read my way through the Collected Works of a dozen or more established poets, as well as several shelves full of individual volumes by less prolific writers, I found that I had been pretty rigorous— which is to say arbitrary—in what I had left out. I could not, for example, find a single poem by Lascelles Abercrombie, Gordon Bottomley, Robert Bridges, John Masefield, John Drinkwater, Alfred Noyes or Edward Shanks—to name only a few of the better known practitioners of the period—that seemed to me worth including. I didn't really expect to. For most of these writers were more or less closely involved with what Cyril Connolly has wittily called 'the explosion of Georgian Marsh-gas'. They belonged to a generation, I mean a poetic generation, whose inherited tradition and technique were utterly at variance with the material which they suddenly found themselves trying to handle. So that whether they wrote in the over-simplified lyric vein now commonly associated with 'Georgian' poetry, or in the prosaic, academic mode that was almost equally popular with pre-1914 poets, they were quite unable to adjust themselves, as many critics have pointed out, to the grim realities of modern war. What men and women were experiencing and feeling, after the holocaust of the Somme if not before, could no longer be given poetic expression by writers whose sensibilities had been conditioned in Edwardian days or earlier, and whose poetic conventions were out-worn even before the war started.

Equally, I did not expect to find anything I wanted in the works of Rudyard Kipling, G. K. Chesterton, Laurence Binyon or Wilfrid Wilson Gibson. But I did. Kipling's *A Drifter off Tarentum* is surely worth a place in any war anthology for its marvellous compression of language; and the savage indignation of his brief 'Epitaphs', or of Chesterton's *Elegy in a Country Churchyard*, seem to me revealing examples of the way in which non-combatants as well as front-line soldiers sublimated their feelings in satirical verse

[14]

of a mordant bitterness. Laurence Binyon and Wilfrid Gibson
are in a different category. Both had some first-hand experi-
ence of the war, but both were poets of very limited range.
Yet each wrote two or three poems which I feel pin down,
despite their limitations of versification and vocabulary,
moments of illumination (I am thinking in particular of
Fetching the Wounded and *Mark Anderson*), and whose sincerity
of feeling transcends the convention in which they were
written. And I nearly included a poem of John Masefield's
called *The Island of Skyros* (where Rupert Brooke was buried)
for the sake of what I thought was its closing couplet until I
discovered that the text I had read was only half the poem,
and that the second stanza was disastrously pathetic. The
second half of the first still seems to me remarkable in its
untypicality, and worth quoting for what should have been
its clinching conclusion:

> So, since we communed here, our bones have been
>   Nearer, perhaps, than they again will be,
> Earth and the worldwide battle lie between,
>   Death lies between, and friend-destroying sea.
> Yet here, a year ago, we talked and stood
> As I stand now, with pulses beating blood.

*   *   *

So much for my criteria and methods of selection. The
question of arrangement presented different difficulties.
There are two obvious ways in which to arrange an an-
thology: chronologically, or alphabetically. But chronologi-
cally by what? A chronological arrangement by date of birth
produces hopeless confusion, the work of young poets who
were killed early in the war coming after, instead of before,
that of older men who were lucky enough to survive longer
or altogether. And to ascertain the precise date of composition
of more than a hundred poems, many of which were written
in the trenches and not published until long afterwards, was
clearly impossible.

An alphabetical arrangement seemed equally unsatis-
factory, not only for the same reason—that Sorley, who was
killed in 1915, would come after Owen, who was killed a
week before the Armistice—but because any anthology of
this nature must inevitably draw heavily on the work of the
half-dozen or so poets whose contribution was by common
consent outstanding. I therefore decided to arrange the
poems in seven sections, each representative of a mood or a
subject connected with the war. This had a double advantage.
It meant that the work of those poets most numerously
represented was dispersed throughout the book, instead of
appearing in a series of solid lumps, and it allowed me to try
to reflect not only the chronological progress of the war, but
also the changing attitude of poets to it. I then arranged the
poems in each section quite arbitrarily, as I thought best,
after taking account of their subject-matter, mood and tone.
Certain juxtapositions seemed to offer helpful contrasts and
comparisons. Thus I think it is interesting to read Herbert
Read's *My Company* immediately after Sassoon's *The Redeemer*,
or Edward Thomas's *A Private* alongside Harold Monro's
Youth in Arms. Each, I think, gains something from the other.

I have called my first section 'Visions of Glory', because
it sets out to represent the mood of optimistic exhilaration
with which so many writers, young and old, greeted the out-
break of war. This was the period of euphoria, when it was
still possible to believe that war was a tolerably chivalrous
affair, offering welcome opportunities for heroism and self-
sacrifice, and to hope that this particular war would be over
in six months. Rupert Brooke's 1914 sonnets are the apo-
theosis of this attitude, and though they seem to me to suffer
from a crippling shallowness of feeling, and to be corre-
spondingly facile in expression, it is undeniable that they said
something to the men who went off to fight, and be killed,
in the early years of the war. As Mr. Bernard Bergonzi has
put it: 'at the time, Brooke seemed to be speaking for his
generation: innumerable young men responded to the war

with feelings that were a compound of traditional patriotism and boredom with the world they had grown up in.' So, despite my reservations, I thought it right to include 'Now, God be thanked Who has matched us with His hour' in this opening section.

But that this mood of exhilaration was capable of finding expression in poems of a very different calibre is, I hope, sufficiently demonstrated by some of the other items in this group—among them, for example, Edward Thomas's *The Trumpet*, Isaac Rosenberg's *Soldier: Twentieth Century*, Siegfried Sassoon's *The Kiss*, and the well-known poem by Thomas Hardy whose title I have borrowed for this book. The Sassoon poem is particularly interesting, not only for its technical accomplishment and for the terrifying image in the final line, but because in spirit it is so completely alien to the author's whole attitude to war. For that reason, Mr. Sassoon was understandably reluctant to let me reprint it, fearing that it might be taken as meant seriously—as a 'fire-eating' poem. 'As a matter of fact', so he told me in subsequent correspondence, 'I originally wrote it as a sort of exercise—in Anglo-Saxon words, as far as I could manage it—after being disgusted by the barbarities of the famous bayonet-fighting lecture. To this day I don't know what made me write it, for I never felt that I could have stuck a bayonet into anyone, even in self-defence. The difficulty is that it doesn't show any sign of satire.' This is true, but it still seems to me a poem of compelling simplicity and power, and a remarkable example of how an 'exercise' can sometimes turn into a work of art. So I am very grateful for permission to include it, and along with it this first-hand account of its origin.

Perhaps the most remarkable of all the poems in this section, though, is Charles Sorley's *All the Hills and Vales Along*. In writing about Sorley in 'The Progress of Poetry' I said that there was 'a magnificent zest about nearly everything he wrote, a zest which is frequently betrayed into naiveté by the inadequacy of his technique.' I was thinking, in part, of this particular poem, and especially of its opening lines:

> 'All the hills and vales along
> Earth is bursting into song,
> And the singers are the chaps
> Who are going to die perhaps.'

Having re-read it many times since, I now think the naiveté was wholly mine, and that this strangely ambivalent poem, with its astringent mixture of joy and bitterness, of the colloquial and the rhetorical, is not only singularly moving but, in its beautifully controlled tone, a technical triumph astonishing in a young man who was only twenty when he was killed.

In the second section one moves from the vision to the reality, from the poetry of exhortation and exhilaration to poems whose basic subject-matter is 'the hell where youth and laughter go'. It is only natural that the poems in this group, with two exceptions, should have been written by men with front-line experience, men who had known at first hand the realities of trench warfare. It is those realities, so appalling in stark fact and so unimaginable by those who had not experienced them, that these poems endeavour to express. Their approach is therefore for the most part factual, their tone objective:

> 'One derelict grim skeleton
> That drench and dry had battened on
> Still seemed to wish us malison;
>
> Still zipped across the gouts of lead
> Or cracked like whipcracks overhead;
> The gray rags fluttered on the dead.'

They set out to make us see with our own eyes 'the gibbet trees like bones or thorns' sticking up between the mud-filled craters of No-Man's-Land, to hear 'the mad gusts tugging on the wire', to understand the tense agony of waiting, during a heavy bombardment, 'for the imminent crash which meant our death', or to realise the horrors of a gas attack.

Not all these poems, however, are horrific. Isaac Rosenberg, in *Returning, We Hear The Larks*, first conveys and then marvellously transmutes 'the sinister threat' that confronts him into a poem of joy at 'heights of night ringing with unseen larks'; Robert Graves uses irony and deliberate understatement to tell the macabre story of Sergeant-Major Money; and Ivor Gurney, another front-line poet, whose work is still too little known, is cool, colloquial, almost detached, in *The Silent One*. But these are exceptions. The truly representative poems in this section—those which achieve the essential documentation but do something more —are Owen's *Exposure*, Sassoon's *A Working Party*, and Blunden's *The Zonnebeke Road*. And of these, Owen's is surely outstanding, not only for the descriptive brilliance of its four opening stanzas, with their richly imaginative metaphors and similes, but for the wonderful transition in the fifth stanza whereby Owen suddenly transports us, in the space of four lines, from the snow-filled trenches of Flanders to some sunny meadow in an English spring:

> 'Pale flakes with fingering stealth come feeling for our
>   faces—
> We cringe in holes, back on forgotten dreams, and
>   stare, snow-dazed,
> Deep into grassier ditches. So we drowse, sun-dozed,
> Littered with blossoms trickling where the blackbird
>   fusses.'

That stanza, with its subtly alliterative combination of precise statement and evocative suggestion, and above all its telescoping inflection from 'snow-dazed' to 'sun-dozed', has always seemed to me incomparable, and something which only a very considerable poet could have achieved.

My third section is called 'No More Jokes', for reasons which are sufficiently obvious. The words are from Sassoon's savage poem *Blighters*, and it is his voice which dominates

[19]

this group. These poems are not 'reports on experience', like those in the previous section, but poems of protest. Their prevailing mood is bitter, satirical. They make their point by comment, not description; whether half-humorously, as in Ivor Gurney's *The Bohemians* and Wilfrid Gibson's *The Question*, or sarcastically as in Arthur Graeme West's searing piece beginning 'God, how I hate you', or cynically as in Kipling's *Mesopotamia*. But satire, of whatever sort, is their essential mode. This is not surprising, for we do not nowadays need psychologists to tell us that one of the basic ways in which human beings seek relief from insupportably nerve-wracking experiences is by satirising them.

In this genre, Sassoon is pre-eminent. Having recently read afresh all his war poems, I found myself increasingly impressed not only by the bite and edge that the satirical poems still possess, but by the range and consistency of his contribution as a whole. As a poet of the 1914 war he was surpassed only by Wilfred Owen, whose growing reputation in the intervening years has tended to eclipse his own. But it should not be forgotten that it was Sassoon whose personal encouragement and practical criticism were crucial to Owen at a decisive stage of his development, who cherished Owen's reputation after he was killed, and who—with Edith Sitwell—prepared the first edition of his poems for publication.

My fourth section is called 'The Pity of War', and, as one would expect, it is both the longest and most varied in the book. Fifteen poets are represented in it, who differ widely in age, experience and technique. It was not necessary to have been in the trenches to appreciate 'the pity war distilled' or to understand, if one had the heart and wit, the larger implications of the conflict. Thus two of the most remarkable poems in this group—Hardy's *I Looked Up From My Writing* and de la Mare's *Motley*—are by older poets who wrote of it at a distance. Both are characteristic, in the sense that they could not have been written by anybody else;

which is perhaps true of all good poems. For who but Hardy
could have written:

> 'Oh, I've been scanning pond and hole
>   And waterway hereabout
> For the body of one with a sunken soul
>   Who has put his life-light out.'

or who but de la Mare:

> 'Mine was not news for child to know,
>   And Death—no ears hath. He hath supped where creep
> Eyeless worms in hush of sleep;
>   Yet, when he smiles, the hand he draws
>   Athwart his grinning jaws—
> Faintly the thin bones rattle . . .'

D. H. Lawrence, another non-combatant, also contributes
two striking poems to this section: *Tommies in the Train* and
Bombardment; the one vividly recapturing, and the other
imaginatively creating, a war-time situation.

But it is still the front-line poets who, understandably, have
most to say on this subject and who interpret it most diversely
and movingly. Here the prevalent mood is meditative and
reflective, rather than assertive or denunciatory. Typical of it
are two gifted but very different poets, Edward Thomas and
Edmund Blunden, who found it possible to construct, out of
their varied experiences, if not 'something upon which to
rejoice' at least something with which to solace themselves
and others: poems like Thomas's *As the Team's Head-Brass* or
Blunden's *Zillebeke Brook*, whose quiet rhythms and perceptive
insights create a sense of pastoral calm which, by antithesis,
make their message all the more effective. And there are
slighter poems, by lesser poets, which nevertheless seemed to
me worth including here, either because, like Richard
Aldington's *In the Trenches*, they attempt (if only partly
successfully) to give new life to an old form, or, like Wilfrid
Gibson's *The Dancers* or Cameron Wilson's *Magpies in
Picardy*, they celebrate, however fleetingly:

'The beauty of the wild green earth
And the bravery of man.'*

In a very different category are the four poems by Isaac
Rosenberg which appear in this section. Technically as
remarkable as anything Owen wrote, they have an origin-
ality of approach, a richness of imagery, and a control of
tone as exceptional as they are individual. I have seen it
said, strangely enough by a University don,† that both Owen
and Rosenberg 'were killed before they had anything to
write about except war, and both have been over-rated
because of the pathos and poignancy of their situation.' An
astonishing pronouncement, in view of the existence of such
deservedly well-known poems of Owen's as *My Shy Hand*,
Shadwell Stair, or the early sonnet *Storm* (to name only a few
of those which have nothing to do with war), and of the fact
that Rosenberg had been publishing poetry since 1912, and
writing it much earlier. In point of fact, out of the 230 odd
pages of poetry in his 'Collected Works' there are only 23
pages of 'Trench Poems': a mere ten per cent. As for their both
being 'over-rated', the reader must judge for himself. So far
as Rosenberg is concerned, I take my stand with Sassoon, who
in his moving Introduction to the 'Collected Works' wrote:

'In reading and re-reading these poems I have been
strongly impressed by their depth and integrity. I have
found a sensitive and vigorous mind energetically interested
in experimenting with language, and I have recognised in
Rosenberg a fruitful fusion between English and Hebrew
culture. Behind all his poetry there is a racial quality,

* Bernard Fergusson in his biography of Lord Wavell ('Wavell:
Portrait of a Soldier') tells an interesting story about the history of
Magpies in Picardy. Apparently when it was reprinted by The Poetry Book
Shop in 1919, the last two verses were omitted. Wavell, it is thought,
restored these from memory when including the poem in his anthology
'Other Men's Flowers'. But I think he may have found them, where I
found them, in Miss Jacqueline Trotter's anthology 'Valour and Vision',
published by Longmans in 1920, where the poem is printed in full.

† Graham Hough, in *The Guardian*, August 7th, 1964.

biblical and prophetic. Scriptural and sculptural are the epithets I would apply to him. His experiments were a strenuous effort for impassioned expression; his imagination had a sinewy and muscular aliveness.'

As for Owen, about whom I shall have a word to say later, it is perhaps enough to refer the reader to the poem *Insensibility*, which closes this section. It seems to me undeniably one of the great poems to have come out of the war, out of any war, not only for the incomparable skill with which the half-rhymes are deployed in a seemingly effortless and inevitable succession, but for the way in which it moves from the particular to the general, from the personal to the universal, in a mounting crescendo of feeling; and yet remains always controlled, beautifully modulated, constantly elaborating its central theme without ever diverging from it or indulging the least hint of rhetoric.

The next two sections deal specifically with casualties, with the wounded and the dead, and perhaps because these poignant subjects provided a sharper emotional focus—stirred deeper feelings in those exposed to them—they contain a higher proportion of achieved poems than do other sections. Not all of them are well known. Ivor Gurney's *To His Love*, F. W. Harvey's *Prisoners*—the best poem on its subject that I know—Frank Sidgwick's *Vision* and Richard Aldington's *Soliloquy*—one of the very few war poems in which an imagist technique is successfully employed—are cases in point. But the established names inevitably predominate. Here are Rosenberg's terrifying *Dead Man's Dump*, Robert Graves' *Last Post*, Sorley's sonnets, Sassoon's *The Death-Bed*, and the great 1918 poems of Owen's maturity.

It is difficult to say anything new or valuable about Owen at this juncture. He has been well served by editors and critics, past and present (it is significant that his three editors have all been fellow poets), and there is little that one can add to what has already been written about him by Edmund Blunden and C. Day Lewis, or to Dr. Welland's detailed and perceptive analysis of his work. More recently his brother Harold, in the first two volumes of a comprehensive account of the Owen family, has given us a revealing first-hand picture of his background, childhood and youth.*

But latterly there has arisen a school of thought which considers the poetry of the 1914 war damagingly limited both in vision and form, and which would deny even Owen a place among the major poets of the English language. According to this view, most recently and very ably propounded by Professor John H. Johnston of the University of West Virginia,† these poets were obsessed with the demoralising conditions of modern warfare, were too close to their experience to be able to see it objectively or order it coherently, and, lacking at once restraint, perspective and any organic sense of relationship with the past, produced work which is for the most part fragmentary, 'personal' in a limiting sense ('a tragic event which is understood only in terms of personal misadventure ceases to be tragic') and devoid of any 'unified imaginative vision'. Restricted to 'the lyric mode', they offer no 'positive, assertive attitude with respect to the values upon which motivation and action are based'. Even Owen, whom Professor Johnston praises discriminatingly for his 'extraordinary sensitivity and his efforts to reconcile that sensitivity to the demands of formal poetic art . . . does not measure up to the vast tragic potentialities of his material'. Only an epic poet could have done that, he claims, and adduces David Jones's *In Parenthesis* as an example.‡

* *Journey From Obscurity*, Memoirs of the Owen Family, by Harold Owen. Oxford University Press, 1963 and 1964.

† *English Poetry of the First World War:* a Study in the Evolution of Lyric and Narrative Form. Princeton, 1964.

‡ It so happens that I had re-read that profoundly original book a short while previously, in the hope of finding in it something suitable for this anthology; but I decided otherwise, partly because to call *In Parenthesis* a 'poem' seems to me to stretch the meaning of the word beyond all reasonable bounds, but mainly because its complex structure is such that extracts divorced from their context lose such a significant degree of force and meaning as to be quite unfair to the work as a whole.

This is a tenable proposition, persuasively argued. But it seems to me to rest on a number of misconceptions, both about the nature of poetry and the work of the particular poets under discussion. The forces which impelled them to write in the lyric or elegiac mode rather than in the epic were, first, the physical conditions under which they were for the most part obliged to write, which were hardly conducive to the creation of long, leisurely, expansive works; secondly, and far more important, their realisation that the epic, with its classical ancestry and time-hallowed associations with the heroic, was the very reverse of a suitable medium for what they had to say. How many epic poems, for that matter, have been written about any war since mediaeval times? One may yet be written about the 1914–18 war, but it seems to me increasingly unlikely.

And is it true that shorter poems, whether lyric or elegiac, are ipso facto incapable of expressing 'the vast tragic potentialities' of modern war? I find it difficult to believe. *Full Fathom Five* is a pure lyric of eight lines only, and Shakespeare's Sonnet beginning 'Being your slave . . .' and George Peele's *A Farewell to Arms* are poems of fourteen and eighteen lines respectively. Their subject matter is the onset of advancing age, the anguish of unrequited love, and death. Large enough subjects, one would have thought, whose tragic potentialities they explore profoundly despite the brevity of their form. In what sense then are they inferior to epic poems dealing with the same subjects? Surely this is a question of *scale*, not of quality?

As to the proposition that First World War poetry was almost exclusively concerned with the plight of the ordinary soldier, who, an insignificant pawn in the movement of armies, was at once too close to actuality and too divorced from responsibility to provide a suitable vehicle for 'the tragic vision', I can only say that I think this view totally misguided. It stems, of course, from Yeats's well-known dictum that 'passive suffering is not a theme for poetry'. By which he presumably meant, not that the suffering recorded in these poems wasn't actively felt, but that the anonymous individual, caught up in a situation which he could neither understand nor control, was not capable of embodying the tragic issues involved. Shakespeare didn't think so, or he would hardly have written the scene in Henry VI, Part 3, in which an anonymous father who has unwittingly killed his son in battle meets an anonymous son who has equally unwittingly killed his father. The scene seems to me essentially tragic, despite its formal Senecan pattern and the highly stylised nature of the verse in which it is written, precisely because it deals with the suffering that wars inflict on individuals, as opposed to factions, armies or nations; and above all on *ordinary* individuals—Thomas Wart, Francis Feeble or Tommy Atkins—as opposed to the princes and nobles (or Five-star Generals) who control and conduct them. Because, in short, it dramatises the fact that it is the common man, the private soldier, who is forced to kill and be killed in them, and who in the long run pays for them either with his life-blood or with a very seared conscience. As such, the scene is a direct precursor of Owen's *Strange Meeting*.

Yeats had no opinion of Owen, as is well known, and excluded him from 'The Oxford Book of Modern Verse' on the grounds that his poetry was 'all blood, dirt and sucked sugar-stick'. When Dorothy Wellesley remonstrated with him he said a good deal more in disparagement of Owen's poetry, in a published letter to her which I would think had better be forgotten, for it does him no credit as a critic. He wouldn't have Rosenberg either, and when I also remonstrated with him, through a mutual friend, he sent back a message that in his opinion Rosenberg's poetry was 'all windy rhetoric'. Perhaps the best answer to these criticisms is to take a careful look at some of the poems, and poets, which Yeats *did* consider worthy of inclusion in his Oxford Book.

The other leg of this argument has to do with 'pity', which by now has become almost a dirty word in discussions of First

World War poetry. Here, ironically enough, Owen himself is partly to blame; for the phrase 'the poetry is in the pity', which occurs in his brief enigmatic draft Preface to the Poems, has been taken from its context to lend support to the view that what these poets were writing about was individual suffering. As such, so the argument runs, their work is narrowly personal, emotionally subjective, and devoid of any valid historical links with the past. It seems to me, on the contrary, that the reverse is true: that at any rate the major poems in this book are poems which 'look before and after', that have their roots in the mainstream of English poetry—in Shakespeare, who wrote of 'pity like a naked new-born babe, striding the blast', in Blake and Hopkins, who also understood the meaning of compassion, (for it is compassion, rather than pity, that informs and inspires them); but which also look forward, in the originality of their form and the directness of their approach, to the poetry that would be written in the years to follow. One has only to look at the extent of Owen's influence on the poets of the thirties to see the truth of this.

As to their being narrowly personal and subjective, how can one say this of *The Death-Bed* or *Insensibility*, of *Strange Meeting* or *Lights Out* or *Recalling War*—to name only a few? The originating impulse may have been a personal experience, the occasion specific and concrete, the context horrific, or comic or tragic; but what matters is the poem that emerges at the end. And you cannot condemn a poem as limitingly subjective just because its origin is tied to a specific event, however 'personal', or we should have to dismiss Jonson's Ode to the memory of Sir Lucius Cary and Sir H. Morison, King's *Exequy on his Wife*, and Tennyson's *In Memoriam* for a start. It is the poet's business to override this, to put such a compulsion on his words that they acquire a universal significance, are related to the eternal verities, not merely to the here and now of existence. Death, sudden untimely death and the grief it brings, is the seed from which many of these poems flower, and it seems to me relatively unimportant whether the cause of it was civil or military, a shipwreck or a gas attack or a pit explosion. The starting point of one of Owen's most remarkable poems (*Miners*) was in fact the latter.

As I see it, what the major poets represented here were writing about was not the plight of the individual, still less their own personal plight. They were concerned with something much larger, something which has been the subject of poetry since time immemorial; with:

> ' . . . whatever mourns in man
> Before the last sea and the hapless stars;
> Whatever mourns when many leave these shores;
> Whatever shares
> The eternal reciprocity of tears.'

Sunt lachrymae rerum. A subject which has inspired some of the most enduring poetry in our language, from Milton's *Lycidas* to Hopkins' 'Margaret are you grieving, over Goldengrove unleaving'. A subject over which, just because they were able to transmute it 'into something rich and strange' despite the terrifying nature of its immediate context, the most gifted of them were able to cast what John Bayley has so aptly called 'a kind of benediction'.* Not all of them of course, and none of them all the time. It would be absurd to claim that. But enough, I hope, to justify the making of this collection, and to give it something more than historical and documentary value.

I.M.P.

* When reviewing Owen's 'Collected Poems' in *The Spectator*, October 4th, 1963.

I

VISIONS OF GLORY

O sing, marching men,
Till the valleys ring again.
Give your gladness to earth's keeping,
So be glad, when you are sleeping.

SORLEY

The Trumpet

Rise up, rise up,
And, as the trumpet blowing
Chases the dreams of men,
As the dawn glowing
The stars that left unlit
The land and water,
Rise up and scatter
The dew that covers
The print of last night's lovers—
Scatter it, scatter it!

While you are listening
To the clear horn,
Forget, men, everything
On this earth newborn,
Except that it is lovelier
Than any mysteries.
Open your eyes to the air
That has washed the eyes of the stars
Through all the dewy night:
Up with the light,
To the old wars;
Arise, arise!

EDWARD THOMAS

'Men Who March Away'

(Song of the Soldiers; September 5, 1914)

What of the faith and fire within us
    Men who march away
    Ere the barn-cocks say
    Night is growing gray,
Leaving all that here can win us;
What of the faith and fire within us
    Men who march away?

Is it a purblind prank, O think you,
    Friend with the musing eye,
    Who watch us stepping by
    With doubt and dolorous sigh?
Can much pondering so hoodwink you!
Is it a purblind prank, O think you,
    Friend with the musing eye?

Nay. We well see what we are doing,
    Though some may not see—
    Dalliers as they be—
    England's need are we;
Her distress would leave us rueing:
Nay. We well see what we are doing,
    Though some may not see!

In our heart of hearts believing
    Victory crowns the just,
    And that braggarts must
    Surely bite the dust,
Press we to the field ungrieving,
In our heart of hearts believing
    Victory crowns the just.

[32]

Hence the faith and fire within us
    Men who march away
    Ere the barn-cocks say
    Night is growing gray,
Leaving all that here can win us;
Hence the faith and fire within us
    Men who march away.

THOMAS HARDY

'All the Hills and Vales Along'

All the hills and vales along
Earth is bursting into song,
And the singers are the chaps
Who are going to die perhaps.
   O sing, marching men,
    Till the valleys ring again.
    Give your gladness to earth's keeping,
    So be glad, when you are sleeping.

Cast away regret and rue,
Think what you are marching to.
Little live, great pass.
Jesus Christ and Barabbas
Were found the same day.
This died, that went his way.
   So sing with joyful breath,
    For why, you are going to death.
    Teeming earth will surely store
    All the gladness that you pour.

Earth that never doubts nor fears,
Earth that knows of death, not tears,
Earth that bore with joyful ease
Hemlock for Socrates,
Earth that blossomed and was glad
'Neath the cross that Christ had,
Shall rejoice and blossom too
When the bullet reaches you.
   Wherefore, men marching
    On the road to death, sing!
    Pour your gladness on earth's head,
    So be merry, so be dead.

From the hills and valleys earth
Shouts back the sound of mirth,
Tramp of feet and lilt of song
Ringing all the road along.
All the music of their going,
Ringing swinging glad song-throwing,
Earth will echo still, when foot
Lies numb and voice mute.
   On, marching men, on
   To the gates of death with song.
   Sow your gladness for earth's reaping,
   So you may be glad, though sleeping.
   Strew your gladness on earth's bed,
   So be merry, so be dead.

CHARLES SORLEY

Soldier: Twentieth Century

I love you, great new Titan!
Am I not you?
Napoleon and Caesar
Out of you grew.

Out of unthinkable torture,
Eyes kissed by death,
Won back to the world again,
Lost and won in a breath,

Cruel men are made immortal,
Out of your pain born.
They have stolen the sun's power
With their feet on your shoulders worn.

Let them shrink from your girth,
That has outgrown the pallid days,
When you slept like Circe's swine,
Or a word in the brain's ways.

ISAAC ROSENBERG

The Kiss*

To these I turn, in these I trust—
Brother Lead and Sister Steel.
To his blind power I make appeal,
I guard her beauty clean from rust.

He spins and burns and loves the air,
And splits a skull to win my praise;
But up the nobly marching days
She glitters naked, cold and fair.

Sweet Sister, grant your soldier this:
That in good fury he may feel
The body where he sets his heel
Quail from your downward darting kiss.

SIEGFRIED SASSOON

* See Introduction p. 17 for a note on this poem.

Into Battle

(Flanders, April 1915)

The naked earth is warm with Spring,
  And with green grass and bursting trees
Leans to the sun's gaze glorying,
  And quivers in the sunny breeze;

And life is colour and warmth and light,
  And a striving evermore for these;
And he is dead who will not fight;
  And who dies fighting has increase.

The fighting man shall from the sun
  Take warmth, and life from the glowing earth;
Speed with the light-foot winds to run,
  And with the trees to newer birth;
And find, when fighting shall be done,
  Great rest, and fullness after dearth.

All the bright company of Heaven
  Hold him in their high comradeship,
The Dog-Star, and the Sisters Seven,
  Orion's Belt and sworded hip.

The woodland trees that stand together,
  They stand to him each one a friend;
They gently speak in the windy weather;
  They guide to valley and ridge's end.

The kestrel hovering by day,
  And the little owls that call by night,
Bid him be swift and keen as they,
  As keen of ear, as swift of sight.

The blackbird sings to him, 'Brother, brother,
  If this be the last song you shall sing,
Sing well, for you may not sing another;
  Brother, sing.'

In dreary, doubtful waiting hours,
  Before the brazen frenzy starts,
The horses show him nobler powers;
  O patient eyes, courageous hearts!

And when the burning moment breaks,
  And all things else are out of mind,
And only joy of battle takes
  Him by the throat, and makes him blind,

Through joy and blindness he shall know,
  Not caring much to know, that still
Nor lead nor steel shall reach him, so
  That it be not the Destined Will.

The thundering line of battle stands,
  And in the air Death moans and sings;
But Day shall clasp him with strong hands,
  And Night shall fold him in soft wings.

JULIAN GRENFELL

Peace

Now, God be thanked Who has matched us with His hour,
And caught our youth, and wakened us from sleeping,
With hand made sure, clear eye, and sharpened power,
To turn, as swimmers into cleanness leaping,
Glad from a world grown old and cold and weary,
Leave the sick hearts that honour could not move,
And half-men, and their dirty songs and dreary,
And all the little emptiness of love!

Oh! we, who have known shame, we have found release
    there,
Where there's no ill, no grief, but sleep has mending,
Naught broken save this body, lost but breath;
Nothing to shake the laughing heart's long peace there
But only agony, and that has ending;
And the worst friend and enemy is but Death.

RUPERT BROOKE

The Volunteer

Here lies a clerk who half his life had spent
Toiling at ledgers in a city grey,
Thinking that so his days would drift away
With no lance broken in life's tournament.
Yet ever 'twixt the books and his bright eyes
The gleaming eagles of the legions came,
And horsemen, charging under phantom skies,
Went thundering past beneath the oriflamme.

And now those waiting dreams are satisfied;
From twilight to the halls of dawn he went;
His lance is broken; but he lies content
With that high hour, in which he lived and died.
And falling thus he wants no recompense,
Who found his battle in the last resort;
Nor need he any hearse to bear him hence,
Who goes to join the men of Agincourt.

HERBERT ASQUITH

The Day's March

The battery grides and jingles,
Mile succeeds to mile;
Shaking the noonday sunshine,
The guns lunge out awhile,
And then are still awhile.

We amble along the highway;
The reeking, powdery dust
Ascends and cakes our faces
With a striped, sweaty crust.

Under the still sky's violet
The heat throbs on the air . . .
The white road's dusty radiance
Assumes a dark glare.

With a head hot and heavy,
And eyes that cannot rest,
And a black heart burning
In a stifled breast,

I sit in the saddle,
I feel the road unroll,
And keep my senses straightened
Toward to-morrow's goal.

There, over unknown meadows
Which we must reach at last,
Day and night thunders
A black and chilly blast.

Heads forget heaviness,
Hearts forget spleen,
For by that mighty winnowing
Being is blown clean.

Light in the eyes again,
Strength in the hand,
A spirit dares, dies, forgives,
And can understand!

And, best! Love comes back again
After grief and shame,
And along the wind of death
Throws a clean flame.

     *   *   *

The battery grides and jingles,
Mile succeeds to mile;
Suddenly battering the silence
The guns burst out awhile.

     .   .   .

I lift my head and smile.

ROBERT NICHOLS

Absolution

The anguish of the earth absolves our eyes
Till beauty shines in all that we can see.
War is our scourge; yet war has made us wise,
And, fighting for our freedom, we are free.

Horror of wounds and anger at the foe,
And loss of things desired; all these must pass.
We are the happy legion, for we know
Time's but a golden wind that shakes the grass.

There was an hour when we were loth to part
From life we longed to share no less than others.
Now, having claimed this heritage of heart,
What need we more, my comrades and my brothers?

SIEGFRIED SASSOON

Virtue

Her breast is cold; her hands how faint and wan!
  And the deep wonder of her starry eyes
  Seemingly lost in cloudless Paradise,
And all earth's sorrows out of memory gone.
Yet sings her clear voice unrelenting on
  Of loveliest impossibilities;
  Though echo only answer her with sighs
Of effort wasted and delights forgone.

Spent, baffled, wildered, hated and despised,
  Her straggling warriors hasten to defeat;
By wounds distracted, and by night surprised,
  Fall where death's darkness and oblivion meet:
Yet, yet: O breast how cold! O hope how far!
Grant my son's ashes lie where these men are!

WALTER DE LA MARE

Thanksgiving

Amazement fills my heart to-night,
Amaze and awful fears;
I am a ship that sees no light,
But blindly onward steers.

Flung toward heaven's toppling rage,
Sunk between steep and steep,
A lost and wondrous fight I wage
With the embattled deep.

I neither know nor care at length
Where drives the storm about;
Only I summon all my strength
And swear to ride it out.

Yet give I thanks; despite these wars,
My ship—though blindly blown,
Long lost to sun or moon or stars—
Still stands up alone.
I need no trust in borrowed spars;
My strength is yet my own.

ROBERT NICHOLS

An Irish Airman Foresees his Death

I know that I shall meet my fate
Somewhere among the clouds above;
Those that I fight I do not hate,
Those that I guard I do not love;
My country is Kiltartan Cross,
My countrymen Kiltartan's poor,
No likely end could bring them loss
Or leave them happier than before.
Nor law, nor duty bade me fight,
Nor public men, nor cheering crowds,
A lonely impulse of delight
Drove to this tumult in the clouds;
I balanced all, brought all to mind,
The years to come seemed waste of breath,
A waste of breath the years behind
In balance with this life, this death.

W. B. YEATS

In Memoriam S.C.W., v.c.
(8 September 1915)

There is no fitter end than this.
   No need is now to yearn nor sigh.
We know the glory that is his,
   A glory that can never die.

Surely we knew it long before,
   Knew all along that he was made
For a swift radiant morning, for
   A sacrificing swift night-shade.

CHARLES SORLEY

II

THE BITTER TRUTH

Agony stares from each gray face

BLUNDEN

Exposure

Our brains ache, in the merciless iced east winds that knive
    us . . .
Wearied we keep awake because the night is silent . . .
Low, drooping flares confuse our memory of the salient . . .
Worried by silence, sentries whisper, curious, nervous,
       But nothing happens.

Watching, we hear the mad gusts tugging on the wire,
Like twitching agonies of men among its brambles.
Northward, incessantly, the flickering gunnery rumbles,
Far off, like a dull rumour of some other war.
       What are we doing here?

The poignant misery of dawn begins to grow . . .
We only know war lasts, rain soaks, and clouds sag stormy.
Dawn massing in the east her melancholy army
Attacks once more in ranks on shivering ranks of gray,
       But nothing happens.

Sudden successive flights of bullets streak the silence.
Less deathly than the air that shudders black with snow,
With sidelong flowing flakes that flock, pause, and renew;
We watch them wandering up and down the wind's non-
    chalance,
       But nothing happens.

Pale flakes with fingering stealth come feeling for our
    faces—
We cringe in holes, back on forgotten dreams, and stare,
    snow-dazed,
Deep into grassier ditches. So we drowse, sun-dozed,
Littered with blossoms trickling where the blackbird fusses.
       Is it that we are dying?

[51]

Slowly our ghosts drag home: glimpsing the sunk fires,
   glozed
With crusted dark-red jewels; crickets jingle there;
For hours the innocent mice rejoice: the house is theirs;
Shutters and doors, all closed: on us the doors are closed,—
     We turn back to our dying.

Since we believe not otherwise can kind fires burn;
Nor ever suns smile true on child, or field, or fruit.
For God's invincible spring our love is made afraid;
Therefore, not loath, we lie out here; therefore were born,
     For love of God seems dying.

To-night, His frost will fasten on this mud and us,
Shrivelling many hands, puckering foreheads crisp.
The burying-party, picks and shovels in their shaking
   grasp,
Pause over half-known faces. All their eyes are ice,
     But nothing happens.

WILFRED OWEN

Returning, *We hear the Larks*

Sombre the night is.
And though we have our lives, we know
What sinister threat lurks there.

Dragging these anguished limbs, we only know
This poison-blasted track opens on our camp—
On a little safe sleep.

But hark! joy—joy—strange joy.
Lo! heights of night ringing with unseen larks.
Music showering on our upturned list'ning faces.

Death could drop from the dark
As easily as song—
But song only dropped,
Like a blind man's dreams on the sand
By dangerous tides,
Like a girl's dark hair for she dreams no
    ruin lies there,
Or her kisses where a serpent hides.

ISAAC ROSENBERG

The Redeemer

Darkness: the rain sluiced down; the mire was deep;
It was past twelve on a mid-winter night,
When peaceful folk in beds lay snug asleep;
There, with much work to do before the light,
We lugged our clay-sucked boots as best we might
Along the trench; sometimes a bullet sang,
And droning shells burst with a hollow bang;
We were soaked, chilled and wretched, every one;
Darkness; the distant wink of a huge gun.

I turned in the black ditch, loathing the storm;
A rocket fizzed and burned with blanching flare,
And lit the face of what had been a form
Floundering in mirk. He stood before me there;
I say that He was Christ; stiff in the glare,
And leaning forward from His burdening task,
Both arms supporting it; His eyes on mine
Stared from the woeful head that seemed a mask
Of mortal pain in Hell's unholy shine.

No thorny crown, only a woollen cap
He wore—an English soldier, white and strong,
Who loved his time like any simple chap,
Good days of work and sport and homely song;
Now he has learned that nights are very long,
And dawn a watching of the windowed sky.
But to the end, unjudging, he'll endure
Horror and pain, not uncontent to die
That Lancaster on Lune may stand secure.

He faced me, reeling in his weariness,
Shouldering his load of planks, so hard to bear.
I say that He was Christ, who wrought to bless

[54]

THE BITTER TRUTH

All groping things with freedom bright as air,
And with His mercy washed and made them fair.
Then the flame sank, and all grew black as pitch,
While we began to struggle along the ditch;
And someone flung his burden in the muck,
Mumbling: 'O Christ Almighty, now I'm stuck!'

SIEGFRIED SASSOON

My Company

Foule! Ton âme entière est debout dans mon corps.

JULES ROMAINS

I

You became
In many acts and quiet observances
A body and a soul, entire.

I cannot tell
What time your life became mine:
Perhaps when one summer night
We halted on the roadside
In the starlight only,
And you sang your sad home-songs,
Dirges which I standing outside you
Coldly condemned.

Perhaps, one night, descending cold
When rum was mighty acceptable,
And my doling gave birth to sensual gratitude.

And then our fights: we've fought together
Compact, unanimous;
And I have felt the pride of leadership.

In many acts and quiet observances
You absorbed me:
Until one day I stood eminent
And I saw you gather'd round me,
Uplooking,
And about you a radiance that seemed to beat
With variant glow and to give
Grace to our unity.

But, God! I know that I'll stand
Someday in the loneliest wilderness,
Someday my heart will cry
For the soul that has been, but that now
Is scatter'd with the winds,
Deceased and devoid.

I know that I'll wander with a cry:
'O beautiful men, O men I loved,
O whither are you gone, my company?'

2

My men go wearily
With their monstrous burdens.

They bear wooden planks
And iron sheeting
Through the area of death.

When a flare curves through the sky
They rest immobile.

Then on again,
Sweating and blaspheming—
'Oh, bloody Christ!'

My men, my modern Christs,
Your bloody agony confronts the world.

3

A man of mine
        lies on the wire.
It is death to fetch his soulless corpse.

A man of mine
        lies on the wire;
And he will rot
And first his lips
The worms will eat.

[57]

It is not thus I would have him kiss'd,
But with the warm passionate lips
Of his comrade here.

4

I can assume
A giant attitude and godlike mood,
And then detachedly regard
All riots, conflicts and collisions.

The men I've lived with
Lurch suddenly into a far perspective;
They distantly gather like a dark cloud of birds
In the autumn sky.

Urged by some unanimous
Volition or fate,
Clouds clash in opposition;
The sky quivers, the dead descend;
Earth yawns.

They are all of one species.

From my giant attitude,
In godlike mood,
I laugh till space is filled
With hellish merriment.

Then again I assume
My human docility,
Bow my head
And share their doom.

HERBERT READ

The Zonnebeke Road

Morning, if this late withered light can claim
Some kindred with that merry flame
Which the young day was wont to fling through space!
Agony stares from each gray face.
And yet the day is come; stand down! stand down!
Your hands unclasp from rifles while you can,
The frost has pierced them to the bended bone?
Why, see old Stevens there, that iron man,
Melting the ice to shave his grotesque chin:
Go ask him, shall we win?
I never liked this bay, some foolish fear
Caught me the first time that I came in here;
That dugout fallen in awakes, perhaps,
Some formless haunting of some corpse's chaps.
True, and wherever we have held the line,
There were such corners, seeming-saturnine
For no good cause.

    Now where Haymarket starts,
That is no place for soldiers with weak hearts;
The minenwerfers have it to the inch.
Look, how the snow-dust whisks along the road,
Piteous and silly; the stones themselves must flinch
In this east wind; the low sky like a load
Hangs over—a dead-weight. But what a pain
Must gnaw where its clay cheek
Crushes the shell-chopped trees that fang the plain—
The ice-bound throat gulps out a gargoyle shriek.
The wretched wire before the village line
Rattles like rusty brambles or dead bine,
And then the daylight oozes into dun;
Black pillars, those are trees where roadways run.
Even Ypres now would warm our souls; fond fool,
Our tour's but one night old, seven more to cool!

O screaming dumbness, O dull clashing death,
Shreds of dead grass and willows, homes and men,
Watch as you will, men clench their chattering teeth
And freeze you back with that one hope, disdain.

EDMUND BLUNDEN

The Silent One

Who died on the wires, and hung there, one of two—
Who for his hours of life had chattered through
Infinite lovely chatter of Bucks accent:
Yet faced unbroken wires; stepped over, and went
A noble fool, faithful to his stripes—and ended.
But I weak, hungry, and willing only for the chance
Of line—to fight in the line, lay down under unbroken
Wires, and saw the flashes and kept unshaken,
Till the politest voice—a finicking accent, said:
'Do you think you might crawl through, there: there's a
    hole'
Darkness, shot at: I smiled, as politely replied—
'I'm afraid not, Sir.' There was no hole, no way to be seen,
Nothing but chance of death, after tearing of clothes
Kept flat, and watched the darkness, hearing bullets
    whizzing—
And thought of music—and swore deep heart's deep
    oaths
(Polite to God) and retreated and came on again,
Again retreated—and a second time faced the screen.

IVOR GURNEY

Sergeant-Major Money
(1917)

It wasn't our battalion, but we lay alongside it,
   So the story is as true as the telling is frank.
They hadn't one Line-officer left, after Arras,
   Except a batty major and the Colonel, who drank.

'B' Company Commander was fresh from the Depôt,
   An expert on gas drill, otherwise a dud;
So Sergeant-Major Money carried on, as instructed,
   And that's where the swaddies began to sweat blood.

His Old Army humour was so well-spiced and hearty
   That one poor sod shot himself, and one lost his wits;
But discipline's maintained, and back in rest-billets
   The Colonel congratulates 'B' company on their kits.

The subalterns went easy, as was only natural
   With a terror like Money driving the machine,
Till finally two Welshmen, butties from the Rhondda,
   Bayoneted their bugbear in a field-canteen.

Well, we couldn't blame the officers, they relied on Money;
   We couldn't blame the pitboys, their courage was
      grand;
Or, least of all, blame Money, an old stiff surviving
   In a New (bloody) Army he couldn't understand.

ROBERT GRAVES

Bombardment

Four days the earth was rent and torn
By bursting steel,
The houses fell about us;
Three nights we dared not sleep,
Sweating, and listening for the imminent crash
Which meant our death.

The fourth night every man,
Nerve-tortured, racked to exhaustion,
Slept, muttering and twitching,
While the shells crashed overhead.

The fifth day there came a hush;
We left our holes
And looked above the wreckage of the earth
To where the white clouds moved in silent lines
Across the untroubled blue.

RICHARD ALDINGTON

The Immortals

I killed them, but they would not die.
Yea! all the day and all the night
For them I could not rest nor sleep,
Nor guard from them nor hide in flight.

Then in my agony I turned
And made my hands red in their gore.
In vain—for faster than I slew
They rose more cruel than before.

I killed and killed with slaughter mad;
I killed till all my strength was gone.
And still they rose to torture me,
For Devils only die for fun.

I used to think the Devil hid
In women's smiles and wine's carouse.
I called him Satan, Balzebub.
But now I call him dirty louse.

ISAAC ROSENBERG

Dulce Et Decorum Est

Bent double, like old beggars under sacks,
Knock-kneed, coughing like hags, we cursed through
   sludge,
Till on the haunting flares we turned our backs
And towards our distant rest began to trudge.
Men marched asleep. Many had lost their boots
But limped on, blood-shod. All went lame; all blind;
Drunk with fatigue; deaf even to the hoots
Of tired, outstripped Five-Nines that dropped behind.

Gas! Gas! Quick, boys!—An ecstacy of fumbling,
Fitting the clumsy helmets just in time;
But someone still was yelling out and stumbling
And flound'ring like a man in fire or lime . . .
Dim, through the misty panes and thick green light,
As under a green sea, I saw him drowning.

In all my dreams, before my helpless sight,
He plunges at me, guttering, choking, drowning.

If in some smothering dreams you too could pace
Behind the wagon that we flung him in,
And watch the white eyes writhing in his face,
His hanging face, like a devil's sick of sin;
If you could hear, at every jolt, the blood
Come gargling from the froth-corrupted lungs,
Obscene as cancer, bitter as the cud
Of vile, incurable sores on innocent tongues,—
My friend, you would not tell with such high zest
To children ardent for some desperate glory,
The old Lie: Dulce et decorum est
Pro patria mori.

WILFRED OWEN

Thiepval Wood

(September 1916)

The tired air groans as the heavies swing over, the river-
    hollows boom;
The shell-fountains leap from the swamps, and with wild-
    fire and fume
    The shoulder of the chalkdown convulses.
Then jabbering echoes stampede in the slatting wood,
Ember-black the gibbet trees like bones or thorns protrude
    From the poisonous smoke—past all impulses.
To them these silvery dews can never again be dear,
Nor the blue javelin-flame of thunderous noons strike fear.

                   EDMUND BLUNDEN

A Working Party

Three hours ago he blundered up the trench,
Sliding and poising, groping with his boots;
Sometimes he tripped and lurched against the walls
With hands that pawed the sodden bags of chalk.
He couldn't see the man who walked in front;
Only he heard the drum and rattle of feet
Stepping along barred trench boards, often splashing
Wretchedly where the sludge was ankle-deep.

Voices would grunt 'Keep to your right—make way!'
When squeezing past some men from the front-line:
White faces peered, puffing a point of red;
Candles and braziers glinted through the chinks
And curtain-flaps of dug-outs; then the gloom
Swallowed his sense of sight; he stooped and swore
Because a sagging wire had caught his neck.

A flare went up; the shining whiteness spread
And flickered upward, showing nimble rats
And mounds of glimmering sand-bags, bleached with rain;
Then the slow silver moment died in dark.
The wind came posting by with chilly gusts
And buffeting at corners, piping thin.
And dreary through the crannies; rifle-shots
Would split and crack and sing along the night,
And shells came calmly through the drizzling air
To burst with hollow bang below the hill.

Three hours ago he stumbled up the trench;
Now he will never walk that road again:
He must be carried back, a jolting lump
Beyond all need of tenderness and care.

THE BITTER TRUTH

He was a young man with a meagre wife
And two small children in a Midland town;
He showed their photographs to all his mates,
And they considered him a decent chap
Who did his work and hadn't much to say,
And always laughed at other people's jokes
Because he hadn't any of his own.

That night when he was busy at his job
Of piling bags along the parapet,
He thought how slow time went, stamping his feet
And blowing on his fingers, pinched with cold.
He thought of getting back by half-past twelve,
And tot of rum to send him warm to sleep
In draughty dug-out frowsty with the fumes
Of coke, and full of snoring weary men.

He pushed another bag along the top,
Craning his body outward; then a flare
Gave one white glimpse of No Man's Land and wire;
And as he dropped his head the instant split
His startled life with lead, and all went out.

SIEGFRIED SASSOON

A Drifter off Tarentum

He from the wind-bitten North with ship and companions
    descended,
Searching for eggs of death spawned by invisible hulls.
Many he found and drew forth. Of a sudden the fishery
    ended
In flame and a clamorous breath known to the eye-pecking
    gulls.

RUDYARD KIPLING

The Sentry

We'd found an old Boche dug-out, and he knew,
And gave us hell, for shell on frantic shell
Hammered on top, but never quite burst through.
Rain, guttering down in waterfalls of slime,
Kept slush waist-high and rising hour by hour,
And choked the steps too thick with clay to climb.
What murk of air remained stank old, and sour
With fumes of whizz-bangs, and the smell of men
Who'd lived there years, and left their curse in the den,
If not their corpses . . .
               There we herded from the blast
Of whizz-bangs, but one found our door at last,—
Buffeting eyes and breath, snuffing the candles,
And thud! flump! thud! down the steep steps came
   thumping
And sploshing in the flood, deluging muck—
The sentry's body; then, his rifle, handles
Of old Boche bombs, and mud in ruck on ruck.
We dredged him up, for killed, until he whined
'O sir, my eyes—I'm blind—I'm blind, I'm blind!'
Coaxing, I held a flame against his lids
And said if he could see the least blurred light
He was not blind; in time he'd get all right.
'I can't,' he sobbed. Eyeballs, huge-bulged like squids',
Watch my dreams still; but I forgot him there
In posting Next for duty, and sending a scout
To beg a stretcher somewhere, and flound'ring about
To other posts under the shrieking air.

*   *   *

Those other wretches, how they bled and spewed,
And one who would have drowned himself for good,—
I try not to remember these things now.
Let dread hark back for one word only: how

[69]

Half listening to that sentry's moans and jumps,
And the wild chattering of his broken teeth,
Renewed most horribly whenever crumps
Pummelled the roof and slogged the air beneath—
Through the dense din, I say, we heard him shout
'I see your lights!' But ours had long died out.

WILFRED OWEN

Festubert: The Old German Line
(May 1916)

Sparse mists of moonlight hurt our eyes
With gouged and scourged uncertainties
Of soul and soil in agonies.

One derelict grim skeleton
That drench and dry had battened on
Still seemed to wish us malison;

Still zipped across the gouts of lead
Or cracked like whipcracks overhead;
The gray rags fluttered on the dead.

EDMUND BLUNDEN

The Marionettes

Let the foul Scene proceed:
   There's laughter in the wings;
'Tis sawdust that they bleed,
   But a box Death brings.

How rare a skill is theirs
   These extreme pangs to show,
How real a frenzy wears
   Each feigner of woe!

Gigantic dins uprise!
   Even the gods must feel
A smarting of the eyes
   As these fumes upsweel.

Strange, such a Piece is free,
   While we Spectators sit,
Aghast at its agony,
   Yet absorbed in it!

Dark is the outer air,
   Coldly the night draughts blow,
Mutely we stare, and stare
   At the frenzied Show.

Yet heaven hath its quiet shroud
   Of deep, immutable blue:
We cry 'An end!' We are bowed
   By the dread, 'It's true!'

While the Shape who hoofs applause
   Behind our deafened ear,
Hoots—angel-wise—'the Cause!'
   And affrights even fear.

        WALTER DE LA MARE

[72]

III

NO MORE JOKES

And there'd be no more jokes in Music-halls
To mock the riddled corpses round Bapaume.

SASSOON

The General

'Good-morning; good-morning!' the General said
When we met him last week on our way to the line.
Now the soldiers he smiled at are most of 'em dead,
And we're cursing his staff for incompetent swine.
'He's a cheery old card,' grunted Harry to Jack
As they slogged up to Arras with rifle and pack.

   . . .

But he did for them both by his plan of attack.

SIEGFRIED SASSOON

The Bohemians

Certain people would not clean their buttons,
Nor polish buckles after latest fashions,
Preferred their hair long, putties comfortable,
Barely escaping hanging, indeed hardly able,
In Bridge and smoking without army cautions
Spending hours that sped like evil for quickness,
(While others burnished brasses, earned promotions).
These were those ones who jested in the trench,
While others argued of army ways, and wrenched
What little soul they had still further from shape,
And died off one by one, or became officers
Without the first of dream, the ghost of notions
Of ever becoming soldiers, or smart and neat,
Surprised as ever to find the army capable
Of sounding 'Lights out' to break a game of Bridge,
As to fear candles would set a barn alight.
In Artois or Picardy they lie—free of useless fashions.

IVOR GURNEY

The Chances

I mind as 'ow the night afore that show
Us five got talkin',—we was in the know.
'Over the top to-morrer; boys, we're for it.
First wave we are, first ruddy wave; that's tore it!'
'Ah well,' says Jimmy,—an' 'e's seen some scrappin'—
'There ain't no more nor five things as can 'appen:
Ye get knocked out; else wounded—bad or cushy;
Scuppered; or nowt except yer feelin' mushy.'
One of us got the knock-out, blown to chops.
T'other was 'urt, like, losin' both 'is props.
An' one, to use the word of 'ypocrites,
'Ad the misfortoon to be took be Fritz.
Now me, I wasn't scratched, praise God Almighty,
(Though next time please I'll thank 'im for a blighty).
But poor young Jim, 'e's livin' an' 'e's not;
'E reckoned 'e'd five chances, an' 'e 'ad;
'E's wounded, killed, and pris'ner, all the lot,
The bloody lot all rolled in one. Jim's mad.

WILFRED OWEN

Batteries out of Ammunition

If any mourn us in the workshop, say
We died because the shift kept holiday.

RUDYARD KIPLING

Vlamertinghe: Passing the Chateau
(July 1917)

'And all her silken flanks with garlands drest'—
But we are coming to the sacrifice.
Must those have flowers who are not yet gone West?
May those have flowers who live with death and lice?
This must be the floweriest place
That earth allows; the queenly face
Of the proud mansion borrows grace for grace
Spite of those brute guns lowing at the skies.

Bold great daisies, golden lights,
Bubbling roses' pinks and whites—
Such a gay carpet! poppies by the million;
Such damask! such vermillion!
But if you ask me, mate, the choice of colour
Is scarcely right; this red should have been much duller.

EDMUND BLUNDEN

Base Details

If I were fierce, and bald, and short of breath,
  I'd live with scarlet Majors at the Base,
And speed glum heroes up the line to death.
  You'd see me with my puffy petulant face,
Guzzling and gulping in the best hotel,
  Reading the Roll of Honour. 'Poor young chap,'
I'd say—'I used to know his father well;
  Yes, we've lost heavily in this last scrap.'
And when the war is done and youth stone dead,
I'd toddle safely home and die—in bed.

SIEGFRIED SASSOON

Elegy in a Country Churchyard

The men that worked for England
They have their graves at home:
And bees and birds of England
About the cross can roam.

But they that fought for England,
Following a falling star,
Alas, alas for England
They have their graves afar.

And they that rule in England,
In stately conclave met,
Alas, alas for England
They have no graves as yet.

G. K. CHESTERTON

Epitaph on an Army of Mercenaries

These, in the day when heaven was falling,
  The hour when earth's foundations fled,
Followed their mercenary calling
  And took their wages and are dead.

Their shoulders held the sky suspended;
  They stood, and earth's foundations stay;
What God abandoned, these defended,
  And saved the sum of things for pay.

A. E. HOUSMAN

The Question

I wonder if the old cow died or not.
  Gey bad she was the night I left, and sick.
Dick reckoned she would mend. He knows a lot—
  At least he fancies so himself, does Dick.

Dick knows a lot. But maybe I did wrong
  To leave the cow to him, and come away.
Over and over like a silly song
  These words keep bumming in my head all day.

And all I think of, as I face the foe
  And take my lucky chance of being shot,
Is this—that if I'm hit, I'll never know
  Till Doomsday if the old cow died or not.

WILFRID WILSON GIBSON

Mesopotamia

(1917)

They shall not return to us, the resolute, the young,
  The eager and whole-hearted whom we gave:
But the men who left them thriftily to die in their own
    dung,
  Shall they come with years and honour to the grave?

They shall not return to us, the strong men coldly slain
  In sight of help denied from day to day:
But the men who edged their agonies and chid them in
    their pain,
  Are they too strong and wise to put away?

Our dead shall not return to us while Day and Night
    divide—
  Never while the bars of sunset hold.
But the idle-minded overlings who quibbled while they
    died,
  Shall they thrust for high employments as of old?

Shall we only threaten and be angry for an hour?
  When the storm is ended shall we find
How softly but how swiftly they have sidled back to power
  By the favour and contrivance of their kind?

Even while they soothe us, while they promise large
    amends,
  Even while they make a show of fear,
Do they call upon their debtors, and take counsel with their
    friends,
  To confirm and re-establish each career?

Their lives cannot repay us—their death could not undo—
   The shame that they have laid upon our race.
But the slothfulness that wasted and the arrogance that
      slew,
   Shall we leave it unabated in its place?

RUDYARD KIPLING

God, How I Hate You

God! how I hate you, you young cheerful men,
Whose pious poetry blossoms on your graves
As soon as you are in them . . .
                       Hark how one chants—
'Oh happy to have lived these epic days'—
'These epic days'! And *he'd* been to France,
And seen the trenches, glimpsed the huddled dead
In the periscope, hung on the rusty wire:
Choked by their sickly foetor, day and night
Blown down his throat: stumbled through ruined hearths,
Proved all that muddy brown monotony
Where blood's the only coloured thing. Perhaps
Had seen a man killed, a sentry shot at night,
Hunched as he fell, his feet on the firing-step,
His neck against the back slope of the trench,
And the rest doubled between, his head
Smashed like an eggshell and the warm grey brain
Spattered all bloody on the parados . . .
Yet still God's in His Heaven, all is right
In this best possible of worlds . . .
God loves us, God looks down on this our strife
And smiles in pity, blows a pipe at times
And calls some warriors home . . .

[84]

NO MORE JOKES

                      How rare life is!
On earth, the love and fellowship of men,
Men sternly banded: banded for what end?
Banded to maim and kill their fellow men—
For even Huns are men. In Heaven above
A genial umpire, a good judge of sport
Won't let us hurt each other! Let's rejoice
God keeps us faithful, pens us still in fold.
Ah, what a faith is ours (almost, it seems,
Large as a mustard seed)—we trust and trust,
Nothing can shake us! Ah how good God is
To suffer us be born just now, when youth
That else would rust, can slake his blade in gore
Where very God Himself does seem to walk
The bloody fields of Flanders He so loves.

ARTHUR GRAEME WEST

Suicide in the Trenches

I knew a simple soldier boy
Who grinned at life in empty joy,
Slept soundly through the lonesome dark,
And whistled early with the lark.

In winter trenches, cowed and glum,
With crumps and lice and lack of rum,
He put a bullet through his brain.
No one spoke of him again.

       .   .   .

You smug-faced crowds with kindling eye
Who cheer when soldier lads march by,
Sneak home and pray you'll never know
The hell where youth and laughter go.

SIEGFRIED SASSOON

The Happy Warrior

His wild heart beats with painful sobs,
His strain'd hands clench an ice-cold rifle,
His aching jaws grip a hot parch'd tongue,
His wide eyes search unconsciously.

He cannot shriek.

Bloody saliva
Dribbles down his shapeless jacket.

I saw him stab
And stab again
A well-killed Boche.

This is the happy warrior,
This is he . . .

HERBERT READ

The Refined Man

I was of delicate mind. I stepped aside for my needs,
Disdaining the common office. I was seen from afar and
    killed. . . .
How is this matter for mirth? Let each man be judged by
    his deeds.
I have paid my price to live with myself on the terms that I
    willed.

RUDYARD KIPLING

Battlefield

The wind is piercing chill
And blows fine grains of snow
Over this shell-rent ground;
Every house in sight
Is smashed and desolate.

But in this fruitless land,
Thorny with wire
And foul with rotting clothes and sacks,
The crosses flourish—
Ci-gît, ci-gît, ci-gît . . .
'Ci-gît 1 soldat Allemand,
Priez pour lui.'

RICHARD ALDINGTON

To the Unknown Warrior

You whom the kings saluted; who refused not
  The one great pleasure of ignoble days,
Fame without name and glory without gossip,
  Whom no biographer befouls with praise.

Who said of you 'Defeated'? In the darkness
  The dug-out where the limelight never comes,
Nor the big drum of Barnum's show can shatter
  That vibrant stillness after all the drums.

Though the time comes when every Yankee circus
  Can use our soldiers for its Sandwich-men,
When those that pay the piper call the tune,
  You will not dance. You will not move again.

You will not march for Fatty Arbuckle,
  Though he have yet a favourable press,
Tender as San Francisco to St. Francis
  Or all the angels of Los Angeles.

They shall not storm the last unfallen fortress,
  The lonely castle where uncowed and free,
Dwells the unkown and undefeated warrior
  That did alone defeat Publicity.

G. K. CHESTERTON

'Blighters'

The House is crammed: tier beyond tier they grin
And cackle at the Show, while prancing ranks
Of harlots shrill the chorus, drunk with din;
'We're sure the Kaiser loves our dear old Tanks!'

I'd like to see a Tank come down the stalls,
Lurching to rag-time tunes, or 'Home, sweet Home',
And there'd be no more jokes in Music-halls
To mock the riddled corpses round Bapaume.

SIEGFRIED SASSOON

IV

THE PITY OF WAR

I mean the truth untold,
The pity of war, the pity war distilled.

OWEN

On Receiving News of the War
(Cape Town, 1914)

Snow is a strange white word.
No ice or frost
Has asked of bud or bird
For Winter's cost.

Yet ice and frost and snow
From earth to sky
This Summer land doth know.
No man knows why.

In all men's hearts it is.
Some spirit old
Hath turned with malign kiss
Our lives to mould.

Red fangs have torn His face.
God's blood is shed.
He mourns from His lone place
His children dead.

O! ancient crimson curse!
Corrode, consume.
Give back this universe
Its pristine bloom.

ISAAC ROSENBERG

Tommies in the Train

The sun shines,,
The coltsfoot flowers along the railway banks
Shine like flat coin which Jove in thanks
Strews each side the lines.

A steeple
In purple elms, daffodils
Sparkle beneath; luminous hills
Beyond—and no people.

England, O Danaë
To this spring of cosmic gold
That falls on your lap of mould!—
What then are we?

What are we
Clay-coloured, who roll in fatigue
As the train falls league after league
From our destiny?

A hand is over my face,
A cold hand.—I peep between the fingers
To watch the world that lingers
Behind, yet keeps pace.

Always there, as I peep
Between the fingers that cover my face!
Which then is it that falls from its place
And rolls down the steep?

Is it the train
That falls like a meteorite
Backward into space, to alight
Never again?

[94]

Or is it the illusory world
That falls from reality
As we look? Or are we
Like a thunderbolt hurled?

One or another
Is lost, since we fall apart
Endlessly, in one motion depart
From each other.

D. H. LAWRENCE

There was a Time

There was a time when this poor frame was whole
And I had youth and never another care,
Or none that should have troubled a strong soul.
Yet, except sometimes in a frosty air
When my heels hammered out a melody
From pavements of a city left behind,
I never would acknowledge my own glee
Because it was less mighty than my mind
Had dreamed of. Since I could not boast of strength
Great as I wished, weakness was all my boast.
I sought yet hated pity till at length
I earned it. Oh, too heavy was the cost!
But now that there is something I could use
My youth and strength for, I deny the age,
The care and weakness that I know—refuse
To admit I am unworthy of the wage
Paid to a man who gives up eyes and breath
For what can neither ask nor heed his death.

EDWARD THOMAS

Glory of Women

You love us when we're heroes, home on leave,
Or wounded in a mentionable place.
You worship decorations; you believe
That chivalry redeems the war's disgrace.
You make us shells. You listen with delight,
By tales of dirt and danger fondly thrilled.
You crown our distant ardours while we fight,
And mourn our laurelled memories when we're killed.
You can't believe that British troops 'retire'
When hell's last horror breaks them, and they run,
Trampling the terrible corpses—blind with blood.
  O German mother dreaming by the fire,
   While you are knitting socks to send your son
   His face is trodden deeper in the mud.

SIEGFRIED SASSOON

'I Looked Up from My Writing'

I looked up from my writing,
   And gave a start to see,
As if rapt in my inditing,
   The moon's full gaze on me.

Her meditative misty head
   Was spectral in its air,
And I involuntarily said,
   'What are you doing there?'

'Oh, I've been scanning pond and hole
   And waterway hereabout
For the body of one with a sunken soul
   Who has put his life-light out.

'Did you hear his frenzied tattle?
   It was sorrow for his son
Who is slain in brutish battle,
   Though he has injured none.

'And now I am curious to look
   Into the blinkered mind
Of one who wants to write a book
   In a world of such a kind.'

Her temper overwrought me,
   And I edged to shun her view,
For I felt assured she thought me
   One who should drown him too.

THOMAS HARDY

Motley

Come, Death, I'd have a word with thee;
And thou, poor Innocency;
And Love—a lad with broken wing;
And Pity, too:
The Fool shall sing to you,
As Fools will sing.

Ay, music hath small sense,
And a tune's soon told,
And Earth is old,
And my poor wits are dense;
Yet have I secrets,—dark, my dear,
To breathe you all. Come near.
And lest some hideous listener tells,
I'll ring my bells.

They are all at war!—
Yes, yes, their bodies go
'Neath burning sun and icy star
To chaunted songs of woe,
Dragging cold cannon through a mire
Of rain and blood and spouting fire,
The new moon glinting hard on eyes
Wide with insanities!

Hush! . . . I use words
I hardly know the meaning of;
And the mute birds
Are glancing at Love
From out their shade of leaf and flower,
Trembling at treacheries

Which even in noonday cower.
Heed, heed not what I said
Of frenzied hosts of men,
More fools than I,
On envy, hatred fed,
Who kill, and die—
Spake I not plainly, then?
Yet Pity whispered, 'Why?'

Thou silly thing, off to thy daisies go.
Mine was not news for child to know,
And Death—no ears hath. He hath supped where creep
Eyeless worms in hush of sleep;
Yet, when he smiles, the hand he draws
Athwart his grinning jaws—
Faintly the thin bones rattle, and—there, there!
Hearken how my bells in the air
Drive away care! . . .

Nay, but a dream I had
Of a world all mad.
Not simple happy mad like me,
Who am mad like an empty scene
Of water and willow tree,
Where the wind hath been;
But that foul Satan-mad,
Who rots in his own head,
And counts the dead,
Not honest one—and two—
But for the ghosts they were,
Brave, faithful, true,
When, head in air,
In Earth's clear green and blue
Heaven they did share
With beauty who bade them there. . . .

THE PITY OF WAR

There, now! Death goes—
Mayhap I've wearied him.
Ay, and the light doth dim,
And asleep's the rose,
And tired Innocence
In dreams is hence. . . .
Come, Love, my lad,
Nodding that drowsy head,
'Tis time thy prayers were said!

WALTER DE LA MARE

Home-thoughts from France

Wan, fragile faces of joy!
Pitiful mouths that strive
To light with smiles the place
We dream we walk alive.

To you I stretch my hands,
Hands shut in pitiless trance
In a land of ruin and woe,
The desolate land of France.

Dear faces startled and shaken,
Out of wild dust and sounds
You yearn to me, lure and sadden
My heart with futile bounds.

ISAAC ROSENBERG

Battery Moving Up to a New Position from Rest Camp: Dawn

Not a sign of life we rouse
In any square close-shuttered house
That flanks the road we amble down
Toward far trenches through the town.

The dark, snow-slushy, empty street. . . .
Tingle of frost in brow and feet. . . .
Horse-breath goes dimly up like smoke.
No sound but the smacking stroke

As a sergeant flings each arm
Out and across to keep him warm,
And the sudden splashing crack
Of ice-pools broken by our track.

More dark houses, yet no sign
Of life. . . . And axle's creak and whine. . . .
The splash of hooves, the strain of trace. . . .
Clatter: we cross the market place.

Deep quiet again, and on we lurch
Under the shadow of a church:
Its tower ascends, fog-wreathed and grim;
Within its aisles a light burns dim. . . .

When, marvellous! from overhead,
Like abrupt speech of one deemed dead,
Speech-moved by some Superior Will,
A bell tolls thrice and then is still.

And suddenly I know that now
The priest within, with shining brow,

Lifts high the small round of the Host.
The server's tingling bell is lost

In clash of the greater overhead.
Peace like a wave descends, is spread,
While watch the peasants' reverent eyes. . . .

The bell's boom trembles, hangs, and dies.

O people who bow down to see
The Miracle of Calvary,
The bitter and the glorious,
Bow down, bow down and pray for us.

Once more our anguished way we take
Towards our Golgotha, to make
For all our lovers sacrifice.
Again the troubled bell tolls thrice.

And slowly, slowly, lifted up
Dazzles the overflowing cup.

O worshipping, fond multitude,
Remember us too, and our blood.

Turn hearts to us as we go by,
Salute those about to die,
Plead for them, the deep bell toll:
Their sacrifice must soon be whole.

Entreat you for such hearts as break
With the premonitory ache
Of bodies, whose feet, hands, and side,
Must soon be torn, pierced, crucified.

Sue for them and all of us
Who the world over suffer thus,

Who have scarce time for prayer indeed,
Who only march and die and bleed.

*   *   *   *

The town is left, the road leads on,
Bluely glaring in the sun,
Toward where in the sunrise gate
Death, honour, and fierce battle wait.

ROBERT NICHOLS

The Sower

(Eastern France)

Familiar, year by year, to the creaking wain
Is the long road's level ridge above the plain.
To-day a battery comes with horses and guns
On the straight road, that under the poplars runs,
At leisurely pace, the guns with mouths declined,
Harness merrily ringing, and dust behind.
Makers of widows, makers of orphans, they
Pass to their burial business, alert and gay.

But down in the field, where sun has the furrow dried,
Is a man who walks in the furrow with even stride.
At every step, with elbow jerked across,
He scatters seed in a quick, deliberate toss,
The immemorial gesture of Man confiding
To Earth, that restores tenfold in a season's gliding.
He is grave and patient, sowing his children's bread:
He treads the kindly furrow, nor turns his head.

LAURENCE BINYON

In the Trenches

Not that we are weary,
Not that we fear,
Not that we are lonely
Though never alone—
Not these, not these destroy us;
But that each rush and crash
Of mortar and shell,
Each cruel bitter shriek of bullet
That tears the wind like a blade,
Each wound on the breast of earth,
Of Demeter, our Mother,
Wound us also,
Sever and rend the fine fabric
Of the wings of our frail souls,
Scatter into dust the bright wings
Of Psyche!

II

Impotent,
How impotent is all this clamour,
This destruction and contest . . .
Night after night comes the moon
Haughty and perfect;
Night after night the Pleiades sing
And Orion swings his belt across the sky.
Night after night the frost
Crumbles the hard earth.

Soon the spring will drop flowers
And patient creeping stalk and leaf
Along these barren lines
Where the huge rats scuttle
And the hawk shrieks to the carrion crow.

THE PITY OF WAR

Can you stay them with your noise?
Then kill winter with your cannon,
Hold back Orion with your bayonets
And crush the spring leaf with your armies!

RICHARD ALDINGTON

'*As the Team's Head-Brass*'

As the team's head-brass flashed out on the turn
The lovers disappeared into the wood.
I sat among the boughs of the fallen elm
That strewed an angle of the fallow, and
Watched the plough narrowing a yellow square
Of charlock. Every time the horses turned
Instead of treading me down, the ploughman leaned
Upon the handles to say or ask a word,
About the weather, next about the war.
Scraping the share he faced towards the wood,
And screwed along the furrow till the brass flashed
Once more.

        The blizzard felled the elm whose crest
I sat in, by a woodpecker's round hole,
The ploughman said. 'When will they take it away?'
'When the war's over.' So the talk began—
One minute and an interval of ten,
A minute more and the same interval.
'Have you been out?' 'No.' 'And don't want to,
    perhaps?'
'If I could only come back again, I should.
I could spare an arm. I shouldn't want to lose
A leg. If I should lose my head, why, so,
I should want nothing more. . . . Have many gone
From here?' 'Yes.' 'Many lost?' 'Yes: good few.
Only two teams work on the farm this year.
One of my mates is dead. The second day
In France they killed him. It was back in March,
The very night of the blizzard, too. Now if
He had stayed here we should have moved the tree.'

'And I should not have sat here. Everything
Would have been different. For it would have been
Another world.' 'Ay, and a better, though
If we could see all all might seem good.' Then
The lovers came out of the wood again:
The horses started and for the last time
I watched the clods crumble and topple over
After the ploughshare and the stumbling team.

EDWARD THOMAS

Futility

Move him into the sun—
Gently its touch awoke him once,
At home, whispering of fields unsown.
Always it woke him, even in France,
Until this morning and this snow.
If anything might rouse him now
The kind old sun will know.

Think how it wakes the seeds,—
Woke, once, the clays of a cold star.
Are limbs, so dear-achieved, are sides,
Full-nerved—still warm—too hard to stir?
Was it for this the clay grew tall?
—O what made fatuous sunbeams toil
To break earth's sleep at all?

WILFRED OWEN

Break of Day in the Trenches

The darkness crumbles away—
It is the same old druid Time as ever.
Only a live thing leaps my hand—
A queer sardonic rat—
As I pull the parapet's poppy
To stick behind my ear.
Droll rat, they would shoot you if they
    knew
Your cosmopolitan sympathies.
Now you have touched this English hand
You will do the same to a German—
Soon, no doubt, if it be your pleasure
To cross the sleeping green between.
It seems you inwardly grin as you pass
Strong eyes, fine limbs, haughty athletes
Less chanced than you for life,
Bonds to the whims of murder,
Sprawled in the bowels of the earth,
The torn fields of France.
What do you see in our eyes
At the shrieking iron and flame
Hurled through still heavens?
What quaver—what heart aghast?
Poppies whose roots are in man's veins
Drop, and are ever dropping;
But mine in my ear is safe,
Just a little white with the dust.

ISAAC ROSENBERG

Beaucourt Revisited

I wandered up to Beaucourt; I took the river track,
And saw the lines we lived in before the Boche went back;
But Peace was now in Pottage, the front was far ahead,
The front had journeyed Eastward, and only left the dead.

And I thought, How long we lay there, and watched across
    the wire,
While the guns roared round the valley, and set the skies
    afire!
But now there are homes in Hamel and tents in the Vale of
    Hell,
And a camp at Suicide Corner, where half a regiment fell.

The new troops follow after, and tread the land we won,
To them 'tis so much hillside re-wrested from the Hun;
We only walk with reverence this sullen mile of mud;
The shell-holes hold our history, and half of them our
    blood.

Here, at the head of Peche Street, 'twas death to show your
    face;
To me it seemed like magic to linger in the place;
For me how many spirits hung round the Kentish Caves,
But the new men see no spirits—they only see the graves.

I found the half-dug ditches we fashioned for the fight
We lost a score of men there—young James was killed that
    night;
I saw the star-shells staring, I heard the bullets hail,
But the new troops pass unheeding—they never heard the
    tale.

I crossed the blood-red ribbon, that once was No Man's
    Land,
I saw a misty daybreak and a creeping minute-hand;

And here the lads went over, and there was Harmsworth
  shot,
And here was William lying—but the new men know them
  not.

And I said, 'There is still the river, and still the stiff, stark
  trees:
To treasure here our story, but there are only these;'
But under the white wood crosses the dead men answered
  low,
'The new men know not Beaucourt, but we are here—we
  know.'

A. P. HERBERT

Zillebeke Brook
(April 1917)

This conduit stream that's tangled here and there
With rusted iron and shards of earthenware,
And tawny-stained with ruin trolls across
The tiny village battered into dross—
This muddy water chuckling in its run
Takes wefts of colour from the April sun,
And paints for fancy's eye a glassy burn
Ribanded through a brake of Kentish fern,
From some top spring beside a park's gray pale,
Guarding a shepherded and steepled dale,
Wherefrom the blue deep-coppiced uplands hear
The dim cool noise of waters at a weir.

And much too clear you bring it back to me,
You dreary brook deformed with cruelty,
Here where I halt to catch the day's best mood,
On my way up to Sanctuary Wood.

EDMUND BLUNDEN

'Therefore is the Name of it called Babel'
(January 1916)

And still we stood and stared far down
Into that ember-glowing town,
Which every shaft and shock of fate
Had shorn unto its base. Too late
  Came carelessly Serenity.

Now torn and broken houses gaze
On to the rat-infested maze
That once sent up rose-silver haze
  To mingle through eternity.

The outlines once so strongly wrought,
Of city walls, are now a thought
Or jest unto the dead who fought . . .
  Foundation for futurity.

The shimmering sands where once there played
Children with painted pail and spade,
Are drearly desolate—afraid
  To meet night's dark humanity,

Whose silver cool remakes the dead,
And lays no blame on any head
For all the havoc, fire, and lead,
  That fell upon us suddenly,

When all we came to know as good
Gave way to Evil's fiery flood,
And monstrous myths of iron and blood
  Seem to obscure God's clarity.

[115]

Deep sunk in sin, this tragic star
Sinks deeper still, and wages war
Against itself; strewn all the seas
With victims of a world disease
—And we are left to drink the lees
Of Babel's direful prophecy.

OSBERT SITWELL

The Sleepers

A battered roof where stars went tripping
  With silver feet,
A broken roof whence rain came dripping,
  Yet rest was sweet.

A dug-out where the rats ran squeaking
  Under the ground,
And out in front the poor dead reeking!
  Yet sleep was sound.

No longer house or dug-out keeping,
  Within a cell
Of brown and bloody earth they're sleeping;
  Oh they sleep well.

Thrice blessed sleep, the balm of sorrow!
  Thrice blessed eyes
Sealed up till on some doomsday morrow
  The sun arise!

F. W. HARVEY

Bombardment

The Town has opened to the sun.
Like a flat red lily with a million petals
She unfolds, she comes undone.

A sharp sky brushes upon
The myriad glittering chimney-tops
As she gently exhales to the sun.

Hurrying creatures run
Down the labyrinth of the sinister flower.
What is it they shun?

A dark bird falls from the sun.
It curves in a rush to the heart of the vast
Flower: the day has begun.

D. H. LAWRENCE

Les Halles d'Ypres

A tangle of iron rods and spluttered beams,
　　On brickwork past the skill of a mason to mend:
A wall with a bright blue poster—odd as dreams
　　Is the city's latter end.

A shapeless obelisk looms Saint Martin's spire,
　　Now a lean aiming-mark for the German guns;
And the Cloth Hall crouches beside, disfigured with fire,
　　The glory of Flanders once.

Only the foursquare tower still bears the trace
　　Of beauty that was, and strong embattled age,
And gilded ceremonies and pride of place—
　　Before this senseless rage.

And still you may see (below the noon serene,
　　The mysterious, changeless vault of sharp blue light),
The pigeons come to the tower, and flaunt and preen,
　　And flicker in playful flight.

EDMUND BLUNDEN

Magpies in Picardy

The magpies in Picardy
Are more than I can tell.
They flicker down the dusty roads
And cast a magic spell
On the men who march through Picardy,
Through Picardy to Hell.

(The blackbird flies with panic,
The swallow goes like light,
The finches move like ladies,
The owl floats by at night;
But the great and flashing magpie
He flies as artists might.)

A magpie in Picardy
Told me secret things—
Of the music in white feathers,
And the sunlight that sings
And dances in deep shadows—
He told me with his wings.

(The hawk is cruel and rigid,
He watches from a height;
The rook is slow and sombre,
The robin loves to fight;
But the great and flashing magpie
He flies as lovers might.)

He told me that in Picardy,
An age ago or more,
While all his fathers still were eggs,
These dusty highways bore
Brown singing soldiers marching out
Through Picardy to war.

[119]

He said that still through chaos
Works on the ancient plan
And two things have altered not
Since first the world began—
The beauty of the wild green earth
And the bravery of man.

(For the sparrow flies unthinking
And quarrels in his flight;
The heron trails his legs behind,
The lark goes out of sight;
But the great and flashing magpie
He flies as poets might.)

T. P. CAMERON WILSON

The Dancers

All day beneath the hurtling shells
Before my burning eyes
Hover the dainty demoiselles—
The peacock dragonflies.

Unceasingly they dart and glance
Above the stagnant stream—
And I am fighting here in France
As in a senseless dream.

A dream of shattering black shells
That hurtle overhead,
And dainty dancing demoiselles
Above the dreamless dead.

WILFRID WILSON GIBSON

Girl to Soldier on Leave

I love you—Titan lover,
My own storm-days' Titan.
Greater than the son of Zeus,
I know whom I would choose.

Titan—my splendid rebel—
The old Prometheus
Wanes like a ghost before your
    power—
His pangs were joys to yours.

Pallid days arid and wan
Tied your soul fast.
Babel-cities' smoky tops
Pressed upon your growth

Weary gyves. What were you
But a word in the brain's ways,
Or the sleep of Circe's swine?
One gyve holds you yet.

It held you hiddenly on the Somme
Tied from my heart at home.
O must it loosen now? I wish
You were bound with the old old gyves.

Love! you love me—your eyes
Have looked through death at mine.
You have tempted a grave too much.
I let you—I repine.

ISAAC ROSENBERG

Concert Party

(Egyptian Base Camp)

They are gathering round . . .
Out of the twilight; over the grey-blue sand,
Shoals of low-jargoning men drift inward to the sound—
The jangle and throb of a piano . . . tum-ti-tum . . .
Drawn by a lamp, they come
Out of the glimmering lines of their tents, over the
   shuffling sand.

O sing us the songs, the songs of our own land,
You warbling ladies in white.
Dimness conceals the hunger in our faces,
This wall of faces risen out of the night,
These eyes that keep their memories of the places
So long beyond their sight.

Jaded and gay, the ladies sing; and the chap in brown
Tilts his grey hat; jaunty and lean and pale,
He rattles the keys . . . some actor-bloke from town . . .
God send you home; and then *A long, long trail;*
I hear you calling me; and *Dixieland.* . . .
Sing slowly . . . now the chorus . . . one by one
We hear them, drink them; till the concert's done.
Silent, I watch the shadowy mass of soldiers stand.
Silent, they drift away, over the glimmering sand.

                              SIEGFRIED SASSOON

Insensibility

I

Happy are men who yet before they are killed
Can let their veins run cold.
Whom no compassion fleers
Or makes their feet
Sore on the alleys cobbled with their brothers.
The front line withers,
But they are troops who fade, not flowers
For poets' tearful fooling:
Men, gaps for filling:
Losses, who might have fought
Longer; but no one bothers.

II

And some cease feeling
Even themselves or for themselves.
Dullness best solves
The tease and doubt of shelling,
And Chance's strange arithmetic
Comes simpler than the reckoning of their shilling.
They keep no check on armies' decimation.

III

Happy are these who lose imagination:
They have enough to carry with ammunition.
Their spirit drags no pack,
Their old wounds, save with cold, can not more ache.
Having seen all things red,
Their eyes are rid
Of the hurt of the colour of blood for ever.
And terror's first constriction over,
Their hearts remain small-drawn.
Their senses in some scorching cautery of battle
Now long since ironed,
Can laugh among the dying, unconcerned.

THE PITY OF WAR

IV

Happy the soldier home, with not a notion
How somewhere, every dawn, some men attack,
And many sighs are drained.
Happy the lad whose mind was never trained:
His days are worth forgetting more than not.
He sings along the march
Which we march taciturn, because of dusk,
The long, forlorn, relentless trend
From larger day to huger night.

V

We wise, who with a thought besmirch
Blood over all our soul,
How should we see our task
But through his blunt and lashless eyes?
Alive, he is not vital overmuch;
Dying, not mortal overmuch;
Nor sad, nor proud,
Nor curious at all.
He cannot tell
Old men's placidity from his.

VI

But cursed are dullards whom no cannon stuns,
That they should be as stones;
Wretched are they, and mean
With paucity that never was simplicity.
By choice they made themselves immune
To pity and whatever mourns in man
Before the last sea and the hapless stars;
Whatever mourns when many leave these shores;
Whatever shares
The eternal reciprocity of tears.

WILFRED OWEN

V

THE WOUNDED

Carry my crying spirit till it's weaned
To do without what blood remained these wounds.

Fetching the Wounded

At the road's end glimmer the station lights;
How small beneath the immense hollow of Night's
Lonely and living silence! Air that raced
And tingled on the eyelids as we faced
The long road stretched between the poplars flying
To the dark behind us, shuddering and sighing
With phantom foliage, lapses into hush.
Magical supersession! The loud rush
Swims into quiet: midnight reassumes
Its solitude; there's nothing but great glooms,
Blurred stars; whispering gusts; the hum of wires.
And swerving leftwards upon noiseless tires
We glide over the grass that smells of dew.
A wave of wonder bathes my body through!
For there in the headlamps' gloom-surrounded beam
Tall flowers spring before us, like a dream,
Each luminous little green leaf intimate
And motionless, distinct and delicate
With powdery white bloom fresh upon the stem,
As if that clear beam had created them
Out of the darkness. Never so intense
I felt the pang of beauty's innocence,
Earthly and yet unearthly.

A sudden-call!

We leap to ground, and I forget it all.
Each hurries on his errand; lanterns swing;
Dark shapes cross and re-cross the rails; we bring
Stretchers, and pile and number them; and heap
The blankets ready. Then we wait and keep
A listening ear. Nothing comes yet; all's still.
Only soft gusts upon the wires blow shrill
Fitfully, with a gentle spot of rain.
Then, ere one knows it, the long gradual train

Creeps quietly in and slowly stops. No sound
But a few voices' interchange. Around
Is the immense night-stillness, the expanse
Of faint stars over all the wounds of France.

Now stale odour of blood mingles with keen
Pure smell of grass and dew. Now lantern-sheen
Falls on brown faces opening patient eyes
And lips of gentle answers, where each lies
Supine upon his stretcher, black of beard
Or with young cheeks; on caps and tunics smeared
And stained, white bandages round foot or head
Or arm, discoloured here and there with red.
Sons of all corners of wide France; from Lille,
Douay, the land beneath the invader's heel,
Champagne, Touraine, the fisher-villages
Of Brittany, the valleyed Pyrenees,
Blue coasts of the South, old Paris streets. Argonne
Of ever smouldering battle, that anon
Leaps furious, brothered them in arms. They fell
In the trenched forest scarred with reeking shell.
Now strange the sound comes round them in the night
Of English voices. By the wavering light
Quickly we have borne them, one by one, to the air,
And sweating in the dark lift up with care,
Tense-sinewed, each to his place. The cars at last
Complete their burden: slowly, and then fast
We glide away.
                    And the dim round of sky,
Infinite and silent, broods unseeingly
Over the shadowy uplands rolling black
Into far woods, and the long road we track
Bordered with apparitions, as we pass,
Of trembling poplars and lamp-whitened grass,
A brief procession flitting like a thought
Through a brain drowsing into slumber; nought

But we awake in the solitude immense!
But hurting the vague dumbness of my sense
Are fancies wandering the night: there steals
Into my heart, like something that one feels
In darkness, the still presence of far homes
Lost in deep country, and in little rooms
The vacant bed. I touch the world of pain
That is so silent. Then I see again
Only those infinitely patient faces
In the lantern beam, beneath the night's vast spaces,
Amid the shadows and the scented dew;
And those illumined flowers, springing anew
In freshness like a smile of secrecy
From the gloom-buried earth, return to me.
The village sleeps; blank walls, and windows barred.
But lights are moving in the hushed courtyard
As we glide up to the open door. The Chief
Gives every man his order, prompt and brief.
We carry up our wounded, one by one.
The first cock crows: the morrow is begun.

LAURENCE BINYON

A Terre
(Being the Philosophy of Many Soldiers)

Sit on the bed. I'm blind, and three parts shell.
Be careful; can't shake hands now; never shall.
Both arms have mutinied against me,—brutes.
My fingers fidget like ten idle brats.

I tried to peg out soldierly,—no use!
One dies of war like any old disease.
This bandage feels like pennies on my eyes.
I have my medals?—Discs to make eyes close.
My glorious ribbons?—Ripped from my own back
In scarlet shreds. (That's for your poetry book.)

A short life and a merry one, my buck!
We used to say we'd hate to live dead-old,—
Yet now . . . I'd willingly be puffy, bald,
And patriotic. Buffers catch from boys
At least the jokes hurled at them. I suppose
Little I'd ever teach a son, but hitting,
Shooting, war, hunting, all the arts of hurting.
Well, that's what I learnt,—that, and making money.

Your fifty years ahead seem none to many?
Tell me how long I've got? God! For one year
To help myself to nothing more than air!
One Spring! Is one too good to spare, too long?
Spring wind would work its own way to my lung,
And grow me legs as quick as lilac-shoots.

My servant's lamed, but listen how he shouts!
When I'm lugged out, he'll still be good for that.
Here in this mummy-case, you know, I've thought
How well I might have swept his floors for ever.

I'd ask no nights off when the bustle's over,
Enjoying so the dirt. Who's prejudiced
Against a grimed hand when his own's quite dust,
Less live than specks that in the sun-shafts turn,
Less warm than dust that mixes with arms' tan?
I'd love to be a sweep, now, black as Town,
Yes, or a muckman. Must I be his load?

O Life, Life, let me breathe,—a dug-out rat!
Not worse than ours the existences rats lead—
Nosing along at night down some safe rut,
They find a shell-proof home before they rot.
Dead men may envy living mites in cheese,
Or good germs even. Microbes have their joys,
And subdivide, and never come to death.
Certainly flowers have the easiest time on earth.
'I shall be one with nature, herb, and stone',
Shelley would tell me. Shelley would be stunned:

The dullest Tommy hugs that fancy now.
'Pushing up daisies' is their creed, you know.
To grain, then, go my fat, to buds my sap,
For all the usefulness there is in soap.
D'you think the Boche will ever stew man-soup?
Some day, no doubt, if . . .

                              Friend, be very sure
I shall be better off with plants that share
More peaceably the meadow and the shower.
Soft rains will touch me,—as they could touch once,
And nothing but the sun shall make me ware.
Your guns may crash around me. I'll not hear;
Or, if I wince, I shall not know I wince.
Don't take my soul's poor comfort for your jest.
Soldiers may grow a soul when turned to fronds,
But here the thing's best left at home with friends.

MEN WHO MARCH AWAY

My soul's a little grief, grappling your chest,
To climb your throat on sobs; easily chased
On other sighs and wiped by fresher winds.

Carry my crying spirit till it's weaned
To do without what blood remained these wounds.

WILFRED OWEN

Casualty

They are bringing him down,
He looks at me wanly.
The bandages are brown,
Brown with mud, red only—
But how deep a red! in the breast of the shirt,
Deepening red too, as each whistling breath
Is drawn with the suck of a slow-filling squirt
While waxen cheeks waste to the pallor of death.

O my comrade!
My comrade that you could rest
Your tired body on mine, that your head might be laid
Fallen and heavy—upon this my breast,
That I might take your hands in my hands
To chafe! That abandoned your body might sink
Upon mine, which here helplessly, grievously stands;
That your body might drink
Warmth from my body, strength from my veins,
Life from my heart that monstrously beats,
Beats, beats and strains
After you vainly!
The trench curves. They are gone.
The steep rain teems down.

O my companion!
Who were you? How did you come,
Looking so wanly upon me? I know—
And O, how immensely long I have known—
Those aching eyes, numb face, gradual gloom,
That depth without groan!
Take now my love—this love which alone
I can give you—and shed without pain—
That life if I could I would succour,
Even as it were
This, this, my poor own!

ROBERT NICHOLS

Mark Anderson

On the low table by the bed
Where it was set aside last night,
Beyond the bandaged lifeless head,
It glitters in the morning light—

And as the hours of morning pass
I cannot sleep, I cannot think,
But only gaze upon the glass
Of water that he could not drink.

WILFRID WILSON GIBSON

Conscious

His fingers wake, and flutter; up the bed.
His eyes come open with a pull of will,
Helped by the yellow may-flowers by his head.
The blind-cord drawls across the window-sill . . .
What a smooth floor the ward has! What a rug!
Who is that talking somewhere out of sight?
Why are they laughing? What's inside that jug?
'Nurse! Doctor!'—'Yes; all right, all right.'

But sudden evening muddles all the air—
There seems no time to want a drink of water,
Nurse looks so far away. And here and there
Music and roses burst through crimson slaughter.
He can't remember where he saw blue sky.
More blankets. Cold. He's cold. And yet so hot.
And there's no light to see the voices by;
There is no time to ask—he knows not what.

WILFRED OWEN

Repression of War Experience

Now light the candles; one; two; there's a moth;
What silly beggars they are to blunder in
And scorch their wings with glory, liquid flame—
No, no, not that,—it's bad to think of war,
When thoughts you've gagged all day come back to scare
    you;
And it's been proved that soldiers don't go mad
Unless they lose control of ugly thoughts
That drive them out to jabber among the trees.

Now light your pipe; look, what a steady hand.
Draw a deep breath; stop thinking; count fifteen,
And you're as right as rain . . .
                                    Why won't it rain? . . .
I wish there'd be a thunder-storm to-night,
With bucketsful of water to sluice the dark,
And make the roses hang their dripping heads.
Books; what a jolly company they are,
Standing so quiet and patient on their shelves,
Dressed in dim brown, and black, and white, and green,
And every kind of colour. Which will you read?
Come on; O *do* read something; they're so wise.
I tell you all the wisdom of the world
Is waiting for you on those shelves; and yet
You sit and gnaw your nails, and let your pipe out,
And listen to the silence: on the ceiling
There's one big, dizzy moth that bumps and flutters;
And in the breathless air outside the house
The garden waits for something that delays.
There must be crowds of ghosts among the trees,—
Not people killed in battle,—they're in France,—
But horrible shapes in shrouds—old men who died
Slow, natural deaths,—old men with ugly souls,

Who wore their bodies out with nasty sins.

*   *   *

You're quiet and peaceful, summering safe at home;
You'd never think there was a bloody war on! . . .
O yes, you would . . . why, you can hear the guns.
Hark! Thud, thud, thud,—quite soft . . . they never
    cease—
Those whispering guns—O Christ, I want to go out
And screech at them to stop—I'm going crazy;
I'm going stark, staring mad because of the guns.

SIEGFRIED SASSOON

Mental Cases

Who are these? Why sit they here in twilight?
Wherefore rock they, purgatorial shadows,
Drooping tongues from jaws that slob their relish,
Baring teeth that leer like skulls' teeth wicked?
Stroke on stroke of pain,—but what slow panic,
Gouged these chasms round their fretted sockets?
Ever from their hair and through their hands' palms
Misery swelters. Surely we have perished
Sleeping, and walk hell; but who these hellish?

—These are men whose minds the Dead have ravished.
Memory fingers in their hair of murders,
Multitudinous murders they once witnessed.
Wading sloughs of flesh these helpless wander,
Treading blood from lungs that had loved laughter.
Always they must see these things and hear them,
Batter of guns and shatter of flying muscles,
Carnage incomparable, and human squander
Rucked too thick for these men's extrication.

Therefore still their eyeballs shrink tormented
Back into their brains, because on their sense
Sunlight seems a blood-smear; night comes blood-black;
Dawn breaks open like a wound that bleeds afresh.
—Thus their heads wear this hilarious, hideous,
Awful falseness of set-smiling corpses.
—Thus their hands are plucking at each other;
Picking at the rope-knouts of their scourging;
Snatching after us who smote them, brother,
Pawing us who dealt them war and madness.

WILFRED OWEN

Prisoners

Comrades of risk and rigour long ago
Who have done battle under honour's name,
Hoped (living or shot down) some meed of fame,
And wooed bright Danger for a thrilling kiss,—
Laugh, oh laugh well, that we have come to this!

Laugh, oh laugh loud, all ye who long ago
Adventure found in gallant company!
Safe in Stagnation, laugh, laugh bitterly,
While on this filthiest backwater of Time's flow
Drift we and rot, till something set us free!

Laugh like old men with senses atrophied,
Heeding no Present, to the Future dead,
Nodding quite foolish by the warm fireside
And seeing no flame, but only in the red
And flickering embers, pictures of the past:—
Life like a cinder fading black at last.

F. W. HARVEY

Disabled

He sat in a wheeled chair, waiting for dark,
And shivered in his ghastly suit of grey,
Legless, sewn short at elbow. Through the park
Voices of boys rang saddening like a hymn,
Voices of play and pleasure after day,
Till gathering sleep had mothered them from him.

*　　*　　*

About this time Town used to swing so gay
When glow-lamps budded in the light blue trees,
And girls glanced lovelier as the air grew dim,—
In the old times, before he threw away his knees.
Now he will never feel again how slim
Girls' waists are, or how warm their subtle hands;
All of them touch him like some queer disease.

*　　*　　*

There was an artist silly for his face,
For it was younger than his youth, last year.
Now, he is old; his back will never brace;
He's lost his colour very far from here,
Poured it down shell-holes till the veins ran dry,
And half his lifetime lapsed in the hot race,
And leap of purple spurted from his thigh.

*　　*　　*

One time he liked a blood-smear down his leg,
After the matches, carried shoulder-high.
It was after football, when he'd drunk a peg,
He thought he'd better join.—He wonders why.
Someone had said he'd look a god in kilts,
That's why; and may be, too, to please his Meg;
Aye, that was it, to please the giddy jilts

THE WOUNDED

He asked to join. He didn't have to beg;
Smiling they wrote his lie; aged nineteen years.
Germans he scarcely thought of; all their guilt,
And Austria's, did not move him. And no fears
Of Fear came yet. He thought of jewelled hilts
For daggers in plaid socks; of smart salutes;
And care of arms; and leave; and pay arrears;
Esprit de corps; and hints for young recruits.
And soon, he was drafted out with drums and cheers.

*　　*　　*

Some cheered him home, but not as crowds cheer Goal.
Only a solemn man who brought him fruits
Thanked him; and then inquired about his soul.

*　　*　　*

Now, he will spend a few sick years in Institutes,
And do what things the rules consider wise,
And take whatever pity they may dole.
To-night he noticed how the women's eyes
Passed from him to the strong men that were whole.
How cold and late it is! Why don't they come
And put him into bed? Why don't they come?

WILFRED OWEN

VI
THE DEAD

None saw their spirits' shadow shake the grass,
Or stood aside for the half used life to pass
Out of those doomed nostrils and the doomed mouth,
When the swift iron burning bee
Drained the wild honey of their youth.

ROSENBERG

The Last Post
(June 1916)

The bugler sent a call of high romance—
'Lights out! Lights out!' to the deserted square:
On the thin brazen notes he threw a prayer,
'God, if it's *this* for me next time in France . . .
O spare the phantom bugle as I lie
Dead in the gas and smoke and roar of guns,
Dead in a row with the other broken ones,
Lying so stiff and still under the sky,
Jolly young Fusiliers, too good to die.'
The music ceased, and the red sunset flare
Was blood about his head as he stood there.

ROBERT GRAVES

A Private

This ploughman dead in battle slept out of doors
Many a frozen night, and merrily
Answered staid drinkers, good bedmen, and all bores:
'At Mrs. Greenland's Hawthorn Bush,' said he,
'I slept.' None knew which bush. Above the town,
Beyond 'The Drover', a hundred spot the down
In Wiltshire. And where now at last he sleeps
More sound in France—that, too, he secret keeps.

EDWARD THOMAS

Youth in Arms: IV
CARRION

It is plain now what you are. Your head has dropped
Into a furrow. And the lovely curve
Of your strong leg has wasted and is propped
Against a ridge of the ploughed land's watery swerve.

You are swayed on waves of the silent ground;
You clutch and claim with passionate grasp of your fingers
The dip of earth in which your body lingers;
If you are not found,
In a little while your limbs will fall apart;
The birds will take some, but the earth will take most
   your heart.

You are fuel for a coming spring if they leave you here;
The crop that will rise from your bones is healthy bread.
You died—we know you—without a word of fear,
And as they loved you living I love you dead.

No girl would kiss you. But then
No girls would ever kiss the earth
In the manner they hug the lips of men:
You are not known to them in this, your second birth.

No coffin-cover now will cram
Your body in a shell of lead;
Earth will not fall on you from the spade with a slam,
But will fold and enclose you slowly, you living dead.

Hush, I hear the guns. Are you still asleep?
Surely I saw you a little heave to reply.
I can hardly think you will not turn over and creep
Along the furrows trenchward as if to die.

HAROLD MONRO

The Death-Bed

He drowsed and was aware of silence heaped
Round him, unshaken as the steadfast walls;
Aqueous like floating rays of amber light,
Soaring and quivering in the wings of sleep.
Silence and safety; and his mortal shore
Lipped by the inward, moonless waves of death.

Someone was holding water to his mouth.
He swallowed, unresisting; moaned and dropped
Through crimson gloom to darkness; and forgot
The opiate throb and ache that was his wound.
   Water—calm, sliding green above the weir.
   Water—a sky-lit alley for his boat,
   Bird-voiced, and bordered with reflected flowers
   And shaken hues of summer; drifting down,
   He dipped contented oars, and sighed, and slept.

Night, with a gust of wind, was in the ward,
Blowing the curtain to a glimmering curve.
Night. He was blind; he could not see the stars
Glinting among the wraiths of wandering cloud;
Queer blots of colour, purple, scarlet, green,
Flickered and faded in his drowning eyes.

Rain—he could hear it rustling through the dark;
Fragrance and passionless music woven as one;
Warm rain on drooping roses; pattering showers
That soak the woods; not the harsh rain that sweeps
Behind the thunder, but a trickling peace,
Gently and slowly washing life away.

.   .   .

He stirred, shifting his body; then the pain
Leapt like a prowling beast, and gripped and tore
His groping dreams with grinding claws and fangs.
    But someone was beside him; soon he lay
    Shuddering because that evil thing had passed.
    And death, who'd stepped toward him, paused
      and stared.

Light many lamps and gather round his bed.
Lend him your eyes, warm blood, and will to live.
Speak to him; rouse him; you may save him yet.
He's young; he hated War; how should he die
When cruel old campaigners win safe through?

But death replied: 'I choose him.' So he went,
And there was silence in the summer night;
Silence and safety; and the veils of sleep.
Then, far away, the thudding of the guns.

SIEGFRIED SASSOON

Two Sonnets

(12 June 1915)

I

Saints have adored the lofty soul of you.
Poets have whitened at your high renown.
We stand among the many millions who
Do hourly wait to pass your pathway down.
You, so familiar, once were strange: we tried
To live as of your presence unaware.
But now in every road on every side
We see your straight and steadfast signpost there.

I think it like that signpost in my land,
Hoary and tall, which pointed me to go
Upward, into the hills, on the right hand,
Where the mists swim and the winds shriek and blow,
A homeless land and friendless, but a land
I did not know and that I wished to know.

II

Such, such is Death: no triumph: no defeat:
Only an empty pail, a slate rubbed clean,
A merciful putting away of what has been.

And this we know: Death is not Life effete,
Life crushed, the broken pail. We who have seen
So marvellous things know well the end not yet.

Victor and vanquished are a-one in death:
Coward and brave: friend, foe. Ghosts do not say
'Come, what was your record when you drew breath?'
But a big blot has hid each yesterday
So poor, so manifestly incomplete.
And your bright Promise, withered long and sped,
Is touched, stirs, rises, opens and grows sweet
And blossoms and is you, when you are dead.

CHARLES SORLEY

To His Love

He's gone, and all our plans
   Are useless indeed.
We'll walk no more on Cotswold
   Where the sheep feed
   Quietly and take no heed.

His body that was so quick
   Is not as you
Knew it, on Severn river
   Under the blue
   Driving our small boat through.

You would not know him now . . .
   But still he died
Nobly, so cover him over
   With violets of pride
   Purple from Severn side.

Cover him, cover him soon!
   And with thick-set
Masses of memoried flowers—
   Hide that red wet
   Thing I must somehow forget.

IVOR GURNEY

For a War Memorial

The hucksters haggle in the mart
The cars and carts go by;
Senates and schools go droning on;
For dead things cannot die.

A storm stooped on the place of tombs
With bolts to blast and rive;
But these be names of many men
The lightning found alive.

If usurers rule and rights decay
And visions view once more
Great Carthage like a golden shell
Gape hollow on the shore,

Still to the last of crumbling time
Upon this stone be read
How many men of England died
To prove they were not dead.

G. K. CHESTERTON

By the Wood

How still the day is, and the air how bright!
A thrush sings and is silent in the wood;
The hillside sleeps dizzy with heat and light;
A rhythmic murmur fills the quietude;
A woodpecker prolongs his leisured flight,
Rising and falling on the solitude.

But there are those who far from yon wood lie,
Buried within the trench where all were found.
A weight of mould oppresses every eye,
Within that cabin close their limbs are bound,
And there they rot amid the long profound,
Disastrous silence of grey earth and sky.

These once, too, rested where now rests but one,
Who scarce can lift his panged and heavy head,
Who drinks in grief the hot light of the sun,
Whose eyes watch dully the green branches spread,
Who feels his currents ever a slowlier run,
Whose lips repeat a silent '. . . Dead! all dead!'

O youths to come shall drink air warm and bright,
Shall hear the bird cry in the sunny wood,
All my Young England fell to-day in fight:
That bird, that wood, was ransomed by our blood!

I pray you when the drum rolls let your mood
Be worthy of our deaths and your delight.

ROBERT NICHOLS

The Dead and the Living One
(1915)

The dead woman lay in her first night's grave,
And twilight fell from the clouds' concave,
And those she had asked to forgive forgave.

The woman passing came to a pause
By the heaped white shapes of wreath and cross,
And looked upon where the other was.

And as she mused there thus spoke she:
'Never your countenance did I see,
But you've been a good good friend to me!'

Rose a plaintive voice from the sod below:
'O woman whose accents I do not know,
What is it that makes you approve me so?'

'O dead one, ere my soldier went,
I heard him saying, with warm intent,
To his friend, when won by your blandishment:

' "I would change for that lass here and now!
And if I return I may break my vow
To my present Love, and contrive somehow

' "To call my own this new-found pearl,
Whose eyes have the light, whose lips the curl
I always have looked for in a girl!"

'—And this is why that by ceasing to be—
Though never your countenance did I see—
You prove you a good good friend to me;

THE DEAD

'And I pray each hour for your soul's repose
In gratitude for your joining those
No lover will clasp when his campaigns close.'

Away she turned, when arose to her eye
A martial phantom of gory dye,
That said, with a thin and far-off sigh:

'O sweetheart, neither shall I clasp you!
For the foe this day has pierced me through,
And sent me to where she is. Adieu!—

'And forget not when the night-wind's whine
Calls over this turf where her limbs recline,
That it travels on to lament by mine.'

There was a cry by the white-flowered mound,
There was a laugh from underground,
There was a deeper gloom around.

THOMAS HARDY

Soliloquy 2

I was wrong, quite wrong;
The dead men are not always carrion.
After the advance,
As we went through the shattered trenches
Which the enemy had left,
We found, lying upon the fire-step,
A dead English soldier,
His head bloodily bandaged
And his closed left hand touching the earth,

More beautiful than one can tell,
More subtly coloured than a perfect Goya,
And more austere and lovely in repose
Than Angelo's hand could ever carve in stone.

RICHARD ALDINGTON

Dead Man's Dump

The plunging limbers over the shattered track
Racketed with their rusty freight,
Stuck out like many crowns of thorns,
And the rusty stakes like sceptres old
To stay the flood of brutish men
Upon our brothers dear.

The wheels lurched over sprawled dead
But pained them not, though their bones
    crunched,
Their shut mouths made no moan.
They lie there huddled, friend and foeman,
Man born of man, and born of woman,
And shells go crying over them
From night till night and now.

Earth has waited for them,
All the time of their growth
Fretting for their decay:
Now she has them at last!
In the strength of their strength
Suspended—stopped and held.

What fierce imaginings their dark souls lit?
Earth! have they gone into you!
Somewhere they must have gone,
And flung on your hard back
Is their soul's sack
Emptied of God-ancestralled essences.
Who hurled them out? Who hurled?

None saw their spirits' shadow shake the grass,
Or stood aside for the half used life to pass
Out of those doomed nostrils and the
   doomed mouth,
When the swift iron burning bee
Drained the wild honey of their youth.

What of us who, flung on the shrieking pyre,
Walk, our usual thoughts untouched,
Our lucky limbs as on ichor fed,
Immortal seeming ever?
Perhaps when the flames beat loud on us,
A fear may choke in our veins
And the startled blood may stop.

The air is loud with death,
The dark air spurts with fire,
The explosions ceaseless are.
Timelessly now, some minutes past,
These dead strode time with vigorous life,
Till the shrapnel called 'An end!'
But not to all. In bleeding pangs
Some borne on stretchers dreamed of home,
Dear things, war-blotted from their hearts.

Maniac Earth! howling and flying, your bowel
Seared by the jagged fire, the iron love,
The impetuous storm of savage love.
Dark Earth! dark Heavens! swinging in
   chemic smoke,
What dead are born when you kiss each
   soundless soul
With lightning and thunder from your
   mined heart,
Which man's self dug, and his blind fingers loosed?

THE DEAD

A man's brains splattered on
A stretcher-bearer's face;
His shook shoulders slipped their load,
But when they bent to look again
The drowning soul was sunk too deep
For human tenderness.

They left this dead with the older dead,
Stretched at the cross roads.

Burnt black by strange decay
Their sinister faces lie,
The lid over each eye,
The grass and coloured clay
More motion have than they,
Joined to the great sunk silences.

Here is one not long dead;
His dark hearing caught our far wheels,
And the choked soul stretched weak hands
To reach the living word the far wheels said,
The blood-dazed intelligence beating for light,
Crying through the suspense of the far torturing wheels
Swift for the end to break
Or the wheels to break,
Cried as the tide of the world broke over his sight.

Will they come? Will they ever come?
Even as the mixed hoofs of the mules,
The quivering-bellied mules,
And the rushing wheels all mixed
With his tortured upturned sight.
So we crashed round the bend,
We heard his weak scream,
We heard his very last sound,
And our wheels grazed his dead face.

ISAAC ROSENBERG

The Farmer

I see a farmer walking by himself
In the ploughed field, returning like the day
To his dark nest. The plovers circle round
In the gray sky; the blackbird calls; the thrush
Still sings-–but all the rest have gone to sleep.
I see the farmer coming up the field,
Where the new corn is sown, but not yet sprung;
He seems to be the only man alive
And thinking through the twilight of this world.
I know that there is war behind those hills,
And I surmise, but cannot see the dead,
And cannot see the living in their midst—
So awfully and madly knit with death.
I cannot feel, but know that there is war,
And has been now for three eternal years,
Behind the subtle cinctures of those hills.
I see the farmer coming up the field,
And as I look, imagination lifts
The sullen veil of alternating cloud,
And I am stunned by what I see behind
His solemn and uncompromising form:
Wide hosts of men who once could walk like him
In freedom, quite alone with night and day,
Uncounted shapes of living flesh and bone,
Worn dull, quenched dry, gone blind and sick, with war;
And they are him and he is one with them;
They see him as he travels up the field.
O God, how lonely freedom seems today!
O single farmer walking through the world,
They bless the seed in you that earth shall reap,
When they, their countless lives, and all their thoughts,
Lie scattered by the storm: when peace shall come
With stillness, and long shivers, after death.

FREDEGOND SHOVE

[162]

'When You see Millions of the mouthless Dead'

When you see millions of the mouthless dead
Across your dreams in pale battalions go,
Say not soft things as other men have said,
That you'll remember. For you need not so.
Give them not praise. For, deaf, how should they know
It is not curses heaped on each gashed head?
Nor tears. Their blind eyes see not your tears flow.
Nor honour. It is easy to be dead.
Say only this, 'They are dead.' Then add thereto,
'Yet many a better one has died before.'
Then, scanning all the o'ercrowded mass, should you
Perceive one face that you loved heretofore,
It is a spook. None wears the face you knew.
Great death has made all his for evermore.

CHARLES SORLEY

The Dead

These hearts were woven of human joys and cares,
  Washed marvellously with sorrow, swift to mirth.
The years had given them kindness. Dawn was theirs,
  And sunset, and the colours of the earth.
These had seen movement, and heard music; known
  Slumber and waking; loved; gone proudly friended;
Felt the quick stir of wonder; sat alone;
  Touched flowers and furs and cheeks. All this is ended.

There are waters blown by changing winds to laughter
And lit by the rich skies, all day. And after,
  Frost, with a gesture, stays the waves that dance
And wandering loveliness. He leaves a white
  Unbroken glory, a gathered radiance,
A width, a shining peace, under the night.

RUPERT BROOKE

Vision

Is it because that lad is dead
   My eyes are doing a double duty,
And drink, for his sake and in his stead,
   Twice their accustomed draught of beauty;

Or does the intoxicating Earth
   Ferment in me with stronger leaven,
Because, for seeing the year's rebirth,
   He loans me eyes that look on heaven?

FRANK SIDGWICK

Asleep

Under his helmet, up against his pack,
After the many days of work and waking,
Sleep took him by the brow and laid him back.
And in the happy no-time of his sleeping,
Death took him by the heart. There was a quaking
Of the aborted life within him leaping . . .
Then chest and sleepy arms once more fell slack.
And soon the slow, stray blood came creeping
From the intrusive lead, like ants on track.

*   *   *

Whether his deeper sleep lie shaded by the shaking
Of great wings, and the thoughts that hung the stars,
High pillowed on calm pillows of God's making
Above these clouds, these rains, these sleets of lead,
And these winds' scimitars;
—Or whether yet his thin and sodden head
Confuses more and more with the low mould,
His hair being one with the grey grass
And finished fields of autumns that are old . . .
Who knows? Who hopes? Who troubles? Let it pass!
He sleeps. He sleeps less tremulous, less cold
Than we who must awake, and waking, say Alas!

WILFRED OWEN

VII

AFTERMATH

But, never, heart, forget:
For this her youngest, best, and bravest died,
These bright dews once were mixed with bloody sweat.

DE LA MARE

Two Fusiliers

And have we done with War at last?
Well, we've been lucky devils both,
And there's no need of pledge or oath
To bind our lovely friendship fast,
By firmer stuff
Close bound enough.

By wire and wood and stake we're bound,
By Fribourt and by Festubert,
By whipping rain, by the sun's glare,
By all the misery and loud sound,
By a Spring day,
By Picard clay.

Show me the two so closely bound
As we, by the wet bond of blood,
By friendship, blossoming from mud,
By Death: we faced him, and we found
Beauty in Death,
In dead men breath.

ROBERT GRAVES

Strange Meeting

It seemed that out of battle I escaped
Down some profound dull tunnel, long since scooped
Through granites which titanic wars had groined.
Yet also there encumbered sleepers groaned,
Too fast in thought or death to be bestirred.
Then, as I probed them, one sprang up, and stared
With piteous recognition in fixed eyes,
Lifting distressful hands as if to bless.
And by his smile, I knew that sullen hall,
By his dead smile I knew we stood in Hell.
With a thousand pains that vision's face was grained;
Yet no blood reached there from the upper ground,
And no guns thumped, or down the flues made moan.
'Strange friend,' I said, 'here is no cause to mourn.'
'None,' said that other, 'save the undone years,
The hopelessness. Whatever hope is yours,
Was my life also; I went hunting wild
After the wildest beauty in the world,
Which lies not calm in eyes, or braided hair,
But mocks the steady running of the hour,
And if it grieves, grieves richlier than here.
For of my glee might many men have laughed,
And of my weeping something had been left,
Which must die now. I mean the truth untold,
The pity of war, the pity war distilled.
Now men will go content with what we spoiled,
Or, discontent, boil bloody, and be spilled.
They will be swift with swiftness of the tigress.
None will break ranks, though nations trek from progress.
Courage was mine, and I had mystery,
Wisdom was mine, and I had mastery:
To miss the march of this retreating world
Into vain citadels that are not walled.
Then, when much blood had clogged their chariot-wheels,

I would go up and wash them from sweet wells,
Even with truths that lie too deep for taint.
I would have poured my spirit without stint
But not through wounds; not on the cess of war.
Foreheads of men have bled where no wounds were.
I am the enemy you killed, my friend.
I knew you in this dark: for so you frowned
Yesterday through me as you jabbed and killed.
I parried; but my hands were loath and cold.
Let us sleep now. . . .'

WILFRED OWEN

Recalling War

Entrance and exit wounds are silvered clean,
The track aches only when the rain reminds.
The one-legged man forgets his leg of wood,
The one-armed man his jointed wooden arm.
The blinded man sees with his ears and hands
As much or more than once with both his eyes.
Their war was fought these twenty years ago
And now assumes the nature-look of time,
As when the morning traveller turns and views
His wild night-stumbling carved into a hill.

What, then, was war? No mere discord of flags
But an infection of the common sky
That sagged ominously upon the earth
Even when the season was the airiest May.
Down pressed the sky, and we, oppressed, thrust out
Boastful tongue, clenched fist and valiant yard.
Natural infirmities were out of mode,
For Death was young again: patron alone
Of healthy dying, premature fate-spasm.

Fear made fine bed-fellows. Sick with delight
At life's discovered transitoriness,
Our youth became all-flesh and waived the mind.
Never was such antiqueness of romance,
Such tasty honey oozing from the heart.
And old importances came swimming back—
Wine, meat, log-fires, a roof over the head,
A weapon at the thigh, surgeons at call.
Even there was a use again for God—
A word of rage in lack of meat, wine, fire,
In ache of wounds beyond all surgeoning.

War was return of earth to ugly earth,
War was foundering of sublimities,
Extinction of each happy art and faith
By which the world had still kept head in air,
Protesting logic or protesting love,
Until the unendurable moment struck—
The inward scream, the duty to run mad.

And we recall the merry ways of guns—
Nibbling the walls of factory and church
Like a child, piecrust; felling groves of trees
Like a child, dandelions with a switch.
Machine-guns rattle toy-like from a hill,
Down in a row the brave tin-soldiers fall:
A sight to be recalled in elder days
When learnedly the future we devote
To yet more boastful visions of despair.

ROBERT GRAVES

Armistice Day

Birds stayed not their singing,
The heart its beating,
The blood its steady coursing
  The child in the dark womb
Stirred; dust settled in the tomb.

Old wounds were still smarting,
Echoes were hollow-sounding,
New desires still upspringing.
  No silent Armistice might stay
Life and Death wrangling in the old way.

Earth's pulse still was beating,
The bright stars circling;
Only our tongues were hushing.
  While Time ticked silent on, men drew
A deeper breath than passion knew.

JOHN FREEMAN

The Cenotaph
(September 1919)

Not yet will those measureless fields be green again
Where only yesterday the wild sweet blood of wonderful
    youth was shed;
There is a grave whose earth must hold too long, too deep
    a stain,
Though for ever over it we may speak as proudly as we
    may tread.
But here, where the watchers by lonely hearths from the
    thrust of an inward sword have more slowly bled,
We shall build the Cenotaph: Victory, winged, with Peace,
    winged too, at the column's head.
And over the stairway, at the foot—oh! here, leave
    desolate, passionate hands to spread
Violets, roses, and laurel, with the small, sweet, twinkling
    country things
Speaking so wistfully of other Springs,
From the little gardens of little places where son or sweet-
    heart was born and bred.
In splendid sleep, with a thousand brothers
            To lovers—to mothers
            Here, too, lies he:
Under the purple, the green, the red,
It is all young life: it must break some women's hearts to
    see
Such a brave, gay coverlet to such a bed!
Only, when all is done and said,
God is not mocked and neither are the dead.
For this will stand in our Market-place—
            Who'll sell, who'll buy
            (Will you or I
Lie each to each with the better grace)?
While looking into every busy whore's and huckster's face

AFTERMATH

As they drive their bargains, is the Face
Of God: and some young, piteous, murdered face.

CHARLOTTE MEW

Peace

Night is o'er England, and the winds are still;
Jasmine and honeysuckle steep the air;
Softly the stars that are all Europe's fill
Her heaven-wide dark with radiancy fair;
That shadowed moon now waxing in the west
Stirs not a rumour in her tranquil seas;
Mysterious sleep has lulled her heart to rest,
Deep even as theirs beneath her churchyard trees.

Secure, serene; dumb now the night-hawk's threat;
The guns' low thunder drumming o'er the tide;
The anguish pulsing in her stricken side. . . .
All is at peace. . . . But, never, heart, forget:
For this her youngest, best, and bravest died,
These bright dews once were mixed with bloody sweat.

WALTER DE LA MARE

1916 seen from 1921

Tired with dull grief, grown old before my day,
I sit in solitude and only hear
Long silent laughters, murmurings of dismay,
The lost intensities of hope and fear;
In those old marshes yet the rifles lie,
On the thin breastwork flutter the grey rags,
The very books I read are there—and I
Dead as the men I loved, wait while life drags

Its wounded length from those sad streets of war
Into green places here, that were my own;
But now what once was mine is mine no more,
I seek such neighbours here and I find none.
With such strong gentleness and tireless will
Those ruined houses seared themselves in me,
Passionate I look for their dumb story still,
And the charred stub outspeaks the living tree.

I rise up at the singing of a bird
And scarcely knowing slink along the lane,
I dare not give a soul a look or word
Where all have homes and none's at home in vain:
Deep red the rose burned in the grim redoubt,
The self-sown wheat around was like a flood,
In the hot path the lizard lolled time out,
The saints in broken shrines were bright as blood.

Sweet Mary's shrine between the sycamores!
There we would go, my friend of friends and I,
And snatch long moments from the grudging wars,
Whose dark made light intense to see them by.
Shrewd bit the morning fog, the whining shots
Spun from the wrangling wire; then in warm swoon
The sun hushed all but the cool orchard plots,
We crept in the tall grass and slept till noon.

EDMUND BLUNDEN

Ypres

She was a city of patience; of proud name,
Dimmed by neglecting Time; of beauty and loss;
Of acquiescence in the creeping moss.
But on a sudden fierce destruction came
Tigerishly pouncing: thunderbolt and flame
Showered on her streets, to shatter them and toss
Her ancient towers to ashes. Riven across,
She rose, dead, into never-dying fame.

White against heavens of storm, a ghost, she is known
To the world's ends. The myriads of the brave
Sleep round her. Desolately glorified,
She, moon-like, draws her own far-moving tide
Of sorrow and memory; toward her, each alone,
Glide the dark dreams that seek an English grave.

LAURENCE BINYON

A Lament

We who are left, how shall we look again
Happily on the sun, or feel the rain,
Without remembering how they who went
Ungrudgingly, and spent
Their all for us, loved, too, the sun and rain?

A bird among the rain-wet lilac sings—
But we, how shall we turn to little things
And listen to the birds and winds and streams
Made holy by their dreams,
Nor feel the heart-break in the heart of things?

WILFRID WILSON GIBSON

The Next War
To Sacheverell
(November 1918)

The long war had ended.
Its miseries had grown faded.
Deaf men became difficult to talk to,
Heroes became bores.
Those alchemists
Who had converted blood into gold
Had grown elderly.
But they held a meeting,
Saying,
'We think perhaps we ought
To put up tombs
Or erect altars
To those brave lads
Who were so willingly burnt,
Or blinded,
Or maimed,
Who lost all likeness to a living thing,
Or were blown to bleeding patches of flesh
For our sakes.
It would look well.
Or we might even educate the children.'
But the richest of these wizards
Coughed gently;
And he said:
  'I have always been to the front
  —In private enterprise—,
  I yield in public spirit
  To no man.
  I think yours is a very good idea
  —A capital idea—
  And not too costly . . .

But it seems to me
That the cause for which we fought
Is again endangered.
What more fitting memorial for the fallen
Than that their children
Should fall for the same cause?'
Rushing eagerly into the street,
The kindly old gentlemen cried
To the young:
    'Will you sacrifice
    Through your lethargy
    What your fathers died to gain?
    The world *must* be made safe for the young!'

And the children
Went. . . .

OSBERT SITWELL

The End

After the blast of lightning from the east,
The flourish of loud clouds, the Chariot Throne;
After the drums of time have rolled and ceased,
And by the bronze west long retreat is blown,

Shall Life renew these bodies? Of a truth
All death will he annul, all tears assuage?—
Or fill these void veins full again with youth,
And wash, with an immortal water, Age?

When I do ask white Age he saith not so:
'My head hangs weighed with snow.'
And when I hearken to the Earth, she saith:
'My fiery heart shrinks, aching. It is death.
Mine ancient scars shall not be glorified,
Nor my titanic tears, the seas, be dried.'

                                        WILFRED OWEN

Lights Out

I have come to the borders of sleep,
The unfathomable deep
Forest where all must lose
Their way, however straight,
Or winding, soon or late;
They cannot choose.

Many a road and track
That, since the dawn's first crack,
Up to the forest brink,
Deceived the travellers,
Suddenly now blurs,
And in they sink.

Here love ends,
Despair, ambition ends,
All pleasure and all trouble,
Although most sweet or bitter,
Here ends in sleep that is sweeter
Than tasks most noble.

There is not any book
Or face of dearest look
That I would not turn from now
To go into the unknown
I must enter and leave alone
I know not how.

The tall forest towers;
Its cloudy foliage lowers
Ahead, shelf above shelf;
Its silence I hear and obey
That I may lose my way
And myself.

EDWARD THOMAS

[182]

In Time of 'The Breaking of Nations'
(1915)

I

Only a man harrowing clods
   In a slow silent walk
With an old horse that stumbles and nods
   Half asleep as they stalk.

II

Only thin smoke without flame
   From the heaps of couch-grass:
Yet this will go onward the same
   Though Dynasties pass.

III

Yonder a maid and her wight
   Come whispering by:
War's annals will fade into night
   Ere their story die.

THOMAS HARDY

INDEX OF FIRST LINES

[184]

[185]

[186]

BIOGRAPHICAL NOTES

ALDINGTON, RICHARD. First attracted attention as an Imagist poet, and with his translations from the classics and French literature. During the second half of the war he saw front-line service in France, where he was severely gassed. After the war wrote several novels, of which the best-known is his war novel *Death of a Hero*, as well as two long poems: *A Fool i' the Forest* (1925) and *A Dream in the Luxembourg* (1930), and several tendentious biographies.

ASQUITH, HERBERT. Barrister son of the Liberal Prime Minister. Served on the Western Front in the Royal Artillery. Author of *The Volunteer and Other Poems* and *Poems 1912–1933*.

BINYON, LAURENCE. Spent the greater part of his life in the British Museum, where in 1932 he became Keeper of the Department of Prints and Drawings. In 1933–4 he was Professor of Poetry at Harvard. During the 1914 war he joined the Red Cross and went to the Front with his unit. A prolific but academic poet throughout his long life, he never wrote so well as when recording some of his personal experiences in France.

BLUNDEN, EDMUND. Poet, critic, and gifted teacher of English, Blunden served as an infantryman almost throughout the war, and was awarded the Military Cross. Was Professor of English Literature in Tokyo 1924–27, and a Fellow of Merton College, Oxford, 1931–44. He shares with Graves and Sassoon the distinction of having written a prose account of the war, *Undertones of War*, as original and moving as his poems. His *Collected Poems* appeared in 1930 and was followed by *Poems 1930–1940*.

BROOKE, RUPERT. Was 27 when the war broke out and had already achieved some reputation in literary circles with his *Poems 1911*, and the thesis on Webster which gained him a Fellowship at King's College, Cambridge. He enlisted at once and enthusiastically, was commissioned in the Royal Naval Division with whom he fought at Antwerp (1914), and died of blood-poisoning in April 1915 en route to Gallipoli. His grave is on the Island of Skyros (see Introduction, p. 15). Brooke's striking good looks, easily appreciated verse, and legendary death epitomised the romantic image of the soldier-poet, and his *1914 and Other Poems* proved a spectacular and lasting best-seller.

CHESTERTON, GILBERT KEITH. Essayist, novelist, poet and Catholic apologist. A Londoner of French-Swiss ancestry, Chesterton began as an artist and cartoonist, studying at the Slade School of Art. A lifelong friend of Hilaire Belloc, he did not actually enter the Roman Church until 1922, but his views had always been essentially Romanist. His poetry, facile but seldom without wit, energy and sincerity, sometimes rises to surprising heights.

DE LA MARE, WALTER. Kentish poet, story-teller, and fantasist, a collateral descendant of Robert Browning. As a clerk in an oil company he published his first book under a pseudonym, but soon established himself as the leading contemporary children's poet. Later he put his incomparable lyric gift to more serious themes. His work, having unfairly suffered the label 'Georgian', is still not fully appreciated: at his best he can be as subtle and moving as any poet of this century. Awarded the Order of Merit in 1953.

FREEMAN, JOHN. Poet, critic and novelist. Freeman's *Collected Poems* embody all the vices but also sometimes the few virtues of 'Georgianism'. He was troubled all his life by a weak heart, but had a highly successful business career, and rose from humble beginnings to be director of a large insurance firm. He was noted for his graceful and humorous conversation and letters.

GIBSON, WILFRID WILSON. A prolific minor poet, whose work has not had quite the attention it deserves. He never practised a profession—apart from war service (he was rejected four times before finally enlisting as a private)—but devoted the whole of his time to poetry. He was a joint-beneficiary of Rupert Brooke's will, and a friend of Siegfried Sassoon.

GRAVES, ROBERT. Son of an Irish poet, and of German-Danish descent on his mother's side. One of the most versatile writers of the 20th century: always primarily a poet, he is also a distinguished novelist, literary critic and mythographer. Spent more time on active duty 1914–1918 than almost any other war poet, and was seriously wounded. His autobiography, *Goodbye to All That*, is one of the most notable books about the Great War.

GRENFELL, JULIAN. Son and heir of Lord Desborough. A professional soldier who had joined the army several years before the war, on leaving Oxford. In France, Grenfell quickly won honours for gallantry, including the D.S.O. He died of wounds early in 1915. *Into Battle* is one of the few poems written by an amateur that have survived the test of time.

GURNEY, IVOR. Gloucestershire born and bred, Gurney is one of the very few English writers who combined the talents of composer and poet. Star pupil of Parry and Vaughan Williams, his songs are still much admired. He saw active service in the ranks from 1916 to the end of the war. The experience shattered his already over-delicate sensibility, and from 1922 until his death he was a patient in mental hospitals. He left many hundreds of poems, most of which are marred by paranoid confusion, but show flashes of great originality and power.

HARDY, THOMAS. Major novelist and poet, born and spent his life in Dorset. He was already 74 when the war broke out. For the first two-thirds of his life he published only novels, although he had always written highly personal poems. As a result of ignorant criticism of the 'pessimism' of his novels, from 1898 until his death he devoted himself to poetry—which was perhaps what he really wanted to do. Few of his poems dealt specifically with the war, but those which did are outstanding.

BIOGRAPHICAL NOTES

HARVEY, F. W. A Gloucestershire solicitor, who lived all his life there except 1914–18. He was a boyhood friend of Ivor Gurney. At the beginning of the war he joined the Gloucestershire Regiment, and won the D.C.M. while a Lance Corporal. Soon afterwards he was commissioned, and then taken prisoner by the Germans. He was in at least seven prison camps. He published *Gloucestershire Friends* in 1917 and *Comrades in Captivity* in 1919.

HERBERT, A. P. London-born barrister and notable campaigner for common sense in law and manners. Served in Gallipoli and France until wounded and invalided out. His memorable novel *The Secret Battle* (Foreword by Winston Churchill) reflects these experiences. Later famous as a contributor to *Punch*, he has written distinguished thrillers, satirical novels, and libretti for musicals. Represented Oxford University in Parliament 1935–1949, where he sponsored good causes too numerous to mention.

HOUSMAN, A. E. An outstanding classical scholar, renowned for the devastating wit of his prefaces and footnotes, who in turn held the Professorship of Latin in the Universities of London and Cambridge. Better known to the general public, however, for his two best-selling collections of lyrics: *A Shropshire Lad* (1896) and *Last Poems* (1922). The 'Epitaph' included here is said to have been prompted by German propaganda that the British armies were hired mercenaries.

KIPLING, RUDYARD. Anglo-Indian imperialist, novelist, short-story writer and poet. Awarded the Nobel Prize 1907. A writer of immense originality and skill, whose work as a whole falls short of greatness through his limited sense of values and his lack of understanding of issues broader than the individual. Not much of his best work was done in verse (though he was offered the Poet Laureateship) and the satirical poems in this anthology are untypical. His only son was killed in action in 1915.

LAWRENCE, D. H. Novelist, poet and critic, was the son of a Nottinghamshire coal-miner. Uniquely gifted, he educated himself by winning scholarships to High School and University, and then took up teaching, but soon abandoned it to devote himself to writing. His early novels, published shortly before the war, quickly won attention from discriminating critics, and were followed by a long sequence of books of every kind, from fiction to poetry. Though very uneven, collectively they demonstrate Lawrence's outstanding genius. He spent the last years of his life abroad, weakened by the tuberculosis which finally killed him, in 1930, at the age of 44. His *Collected Poems*, largely composed in free verse, appeared in 1932.

MEW, CHARLOTTE. A highly original poet whose best work will not be forgotten. She was born in London of relatively well-to-do parents, but her father's death in 1898 left her family in straitened circumstances. She had some literary success in early life with short stories and articles, and did not begin to write poetry until later. She was unable to sustain the death of her sister in 1928, and killed herself in the following year.

[189]

MONRO, HAROLD. Best (and rightly) remembered as the founder and presiding genius of The Poetry Bookshop, Monro was single-mindedly devoted to the dissemination of poetry. It was under his aegis that Edward Marsh's 'Georgian' anthologies were issued, and that many young poets, of varying distinction, first saw print. Monro's taste was disarmingly catholic, but he was an early admirer of Hopkins and T. S. Eliot, and the latter contributed an Introduction to his *Collected Poems* (1933).

NICHOLS, ROBERT. A young Georgian poet who fought in France with the Royal Artillery (see the poem on p. 42) until invalided out after the Battle of the Somme with shell-shock, from which he never wholly recovered. A friend of Graves and Sassoon, through whom he met Owen. After the war Nichols went to Tokyo as Professor of English Literature, and continued to write occasional poems and plays, but never succeeded in recapturing the poignant quality of *Ardours and Endurances* (1917) from which these poems are taken.

OWEN, WILFRED. Now almost universally recognised as the most original and important poet of the period. Though born in Oswestry, near the Welsh border, and with a Welsh name, he was not in fact Welsh. Keenly interested in literature from an early age, Owen's apprentice work was much influenced by Keats. In 1913–15 he tutored in Bordeaux, where his introduction to contemporary French poetry probably inspired his passionate interest in technical innovation. He enlisted in October 1915, and was commissioned in the Manchester Regiment June 1916. Sailed for France at the end of December and spent the appalling winter of 1916–17 mainly in the trenches. In June he was posted home on sick-leave and sent to Craiglockart hospital, near Edinburgh, where he met Sassoon, whose influence had a profound effect on him. In November he rejoined a reserve battalion of his regiment, and returned to France for active service on 1st September 1918. A month later he was awarded the M.C. "for conspicuous gallantry and devotion to duty." He was killed in action on November 4th, a week before the Armistice. A definitive edition of his poems, with an Introduction by C. Day Lewis and a Memoir by Edmund Blunden, was published in 1963.

READ, HERBERT. Yorkshire poet and influential critic of literature and art. He served for four years as a Captain in the Yorkshire Regiment, and won the D.S.O. and M.C. His whole critical life has been devoted to an attempted reconciliation of classicism and romanticism, but he has remained an ultra-romantic in spite of himself. He is a passionate adherent of free verse, see *Collected Poems* (1946).

ROSENBERG, ISAAC. Was born in Bristol of Jewish parents, who moved to London when he was 7. Left school at 14 and was apprenticed as an engraver, attending Art School in the evenings. Decided to make painting his career, and went to the Slade School 1911–14, where he proved a gifted student. Had already begun writing poetry, and in 1912 published *Night and Day*. Told that his lungs were weak, he went to South Africa in June 1914 (see poem on p. 93) but returned the following year and shortly afterwards enlisted, though totally unfitted for military service. Early in 1916 he was sent to France, and on April 1st 1918 he was killed in action. A selection of his poems made by Gordon Bottomley, with a Memoir by Laurence Binyon, appeared in 1922, and his *Collected Poems* in 1949. Siegfried Sassoon wrote a Foreword to the latter, in which he saluted Rosenberg's unique contribution to modern poetry.

SASSOON, SIEGFRIED. Began his literary career as something of a dilettante. In 1913 he published *The Daffodil Murderer*, a clever parody of Masefield. It was the war, however, that brought out his real poetic talent. As an infantry officer in France he soon distinguished himself by wild and heroic exploits (he won an M.C.), but ended as an outspoken pacifist and the author of some of the most savagely satirical anti-war poems ever written (*Counter Attack*, 1918). After the war he produced his famous fictionalised autobiographies, *Memoirs of a Fox-Hunting Man* and *Memoirs of an Infantry Officer*, followed by his war reminiscences *Siegfried's Journey*. His *Collected Poems* appeared in 1947.

SHOVE, FREDEGOND. Was the daughter of the historian F. W. Maitland, Fellow of Trinity College, Cambridge, and Professor of English Law. Following his early death, his widow married the great Charles Darwin's son Francis, and Fredegond thus became step-sister to Bernard Darwin and Frances Cornford. She married Gerald Shove, a Cambridge classical scholar, and spent most of her life in or near the University.

SIDGWICK, FRANK. Born at Rugby. Educated at Rugby and Trinity College, Cambridge, where he won the Chancellor's Medal for English verse. After Cambridge went into partnership with A. H. Bullen, and was in charge of the Shakespeare Head Press. In 1906 founded the publishing firm of Sidgwick & Jackson. Served in the army during the war but never went abroad. Published one distinguished novel and two collections of verse.

SITWELL, OSBERT. Son of Sir George Sitwell, 4th Baronet, and brother of Sacheverell and Edith. After leaving Eton joined the Grenadier Guards (1912–19) and saw active service in France. Admired by Owen, who sent him his poems. Novelist and short-story writer as well as poet and author of a four-volume autobiography, Osbert Sitwell is primarily a satirist—irony being his chief weapon–of bumbledom, stupidity and cruelty.

SORLEY, CHARLES. Was of Scottish descent on both sides. He spent his childhood in Cambridge, where his father was a Professor, and in Wiltshire, where he was educated. The countryside of both counties strongly influenced his poetry. Upon leaving school he spent six months in Germany, and was nearly trapped there by the outbreak of war. He enlisted at once, was commissioned in the Suffolk Regiment, and crossed to France in May 1915. The following October, aged 20, he was killed in the Battle of Loos. *Marlborough and Other Poems*, published in January 1916, ran through six editions that year and has been repeatedly reprinted since. It reveals Sorley as a poet of marked individuality and, for his age, extraordinary maturity of mind.

THOMAS, EDWARD. Born in London of Welsh parents, Thomas won a history scholarship at Oxford and while still an undergraduate married Helen Noble. Her understanding and encouragement of his literary ambitions were crucial during the early years of their marriage, when Thomas was obliged to write for a living more often than pleasure. Up to 1914 he wrote almost entirely prose, the best of which—like his poetry—reflected with subtle artistry his love of the English countryside, but after meeting Robert Frost he turned his attention to verse and some consider he surpassed his master. Thomas enlisted in 1915 and went on active service early in 1917, although he was then nearly 40. He was killed at Arras that April. His *Collected Poems* have a perceptive Foreword by de la Mare, but are still largely undervalued by those who associate Thomas with the Georgians, with whom he has nothing in common.

WEST, ARTHUR GRAEME. Won scholarships to public school and Oxford, where he still was when war broke out. Applied for a commission at Christmas but was rejected because of his eyes, so enlisted in the ranks. Served in France November 1915–March 1916; did officer training in Scotland till August 1916; underwent a spiritual crisis which changed his whole attitude to war, but accepted a commission in September and returned to France, where he was killed by a sniper's bullet in April 1917. His *Diary of a Dead Officer* appeared in 1918, edited by the philosopher C. E. M. Joad.

WILSON, T. P. CAMERON. "A young, unknown schoolmaster, he joined the Sherwood Foresters, and quickly rose to the rank of Captain. He was killed in action in the Somme Valley, March 23, 1918. *Magpies in Picardy*, and other war verse, was published by Harold Monro and 'The Poetry Bookshop' " (from Brian Gardner: *Up the Line to Death, The War Poets 1914–1918*, Methuen & Co., 1964).

YEATS, W. B. Dublin-born poet and dramatist. Began as a minor celtic twilight poet, associated with 'decadent' 'nineties poets such as Dowson and Lionel Johnson. Later met Ezra Pound and soon became the acknowledged leader of the Irish literary renaissance. In middle life became increasingly interested in the occult, while his poetry steadily developed in complexity, depth and power. Awarded Nobel Prize 1923. His last poems are regarded by most critics as the greatest ever produced by a poet in old age.